GLOBALVIEWPOINTS

Biodiversity

DATE DUE

Other Books of Related Interest:

At Issue Series

Global Viewpoints Series

Opposing Viewpoints Series

GLOBALVIEWPOINTS

Biodiversity

Noah Berlatsky, Book Editor

GREENHAVEN PRESS
A part of Gale, Cengage Learning

GALE
CENGAGE Learning

Detroit • New York • San Francisco • New Haven, Conn • Waterville, Maine • London

Elizabeth Des Chenes, *Director, Content Strategy*
Cynthia Sanner, *Publisher*
Douglas Dentino, *Manager, New Product*

For more information, contact:
Greenhaven Press
27500 Drake Rd.
Farmington Hills, MI 48331-3535
Or you can visit our Internet site at gale.cengage.com

Articles in Greenhaven Press anthologies are often edited for length to meet page requirements. In addition, original titles of these works are changed to clearly present the main thesis and to explicitly indicate the author's opinion. Every effort is made to ensure that Greenhaven Press accurately reflects the original intent of the authors. Every effort has been made to trace the owners of copyrighted material.

Cover image © Michele Westmoreland/Corbis.

LIBRARY OF CONGRESS CATALOGING-IN-PUBLICATION DATA

Biodiversity / Noah Berlatsky, book editor.
        pages cm. -- (Global viewpoints)
    Includes bibliographical references and index.
    ISBN 978-0-7377-6904-3 (hardcover) -- ISBN 978-0-7377-6905-0 (pbk.)
    1. Biodiversity. I. Berlatsky, Noah, editor of compilation.
    QH541.15.B56B5645 2013
    333.95--dc23
                                                                2013009180

Printed in the United States of America
1 2 3 4 5   17 16 15 14 13

Contents

The question of whether hunting can be balanced with biodiversity is controversial. Local people and their hunting interests must be included in any discussion of conservation.

Chapter 3: Biodiversity and Agriculture

Chapter 4: Biodiversity and Climate Change

Jamaica is known for its biodiversity. However, its species are threatened by numerous dangers, including deforestation and climate change.

Foreword

*"The problems of all of humanity can
only be solved by all of humanity."*
—*Swiss author Friedrich Dürrenmatt*

Global interdependence has become an undeniable reality. Mass media and technology have increased worldwide access to information and created a society of global citizens. Understanding and navigating this global community is a challenge, requiring a high degree of information literacy and a new level of learning sophistication.

Building on the success of its flagship series, Opposing Viewpoints, Greenhaven Press has created the Global Viewpoints series to examine a broad range of current, often controversial topics of worldwide importance from a variety of international perspectives. Providing students and other readers with the information they need to explore global connections and think critically about worldwide implications, each Global Viewpoints volume offers a panoramic view of a topic of widespread significance.

Drugs, famine, immigration—a broad, international treatment is essential to do justice to social, environmental, health, and political issues such as these. Junior high, high school, and early college students, as well as general readers, can all use Global Viewpoints anthologies to discern the complexities relating to each issue. Readers will be able to examine unique national perspectives while, at the same time, appreciating the interconnectedness that global priorities bring to all nations and cultures.

Material in each volume is selected from a diverse range of sources, including journals, magazines, newspapers, nonfiction books, speeches, government documents, pamphlets, organization newsletters, and position papers. Global Viewpoints is truly global, with material drawn primarily from international sources available in English and secondarily from US sources with extensive international coverage.

Features of each volume in the Global Viewpoints series include:

- An **annotated table of contents** that provides a brief summary of each essay in the volume, including the name of the country or area covered in the essay.

- An **introduction** specific to the volume topic.

- A **world map** to help readers locate the countries or areas covered in the essays.

- For each viewpoint, an **introduction** that contains notes about the author and source of the viewpoint explains why material from the specific country is being presented, summarizes the main points of the viewpoint, and offers three **guided reading questions** to aid in understanding and comprehension.

- **For further discussion** questions that promote critical thinking by asking the reader to compare and contrast aspects of the viewpoints or draw conclusions about perspectives and arguments.

- A worldwide list of **organizations to contact** for readers seeking additional information.

- A **periodical bibliography** for each chapter and a **bibliography of books** on the volume topic to aid in further research.

- A comprehensive **subject index** to offer access to people, places, events, and subjects cited in the text, with the countries covered in the viewpoints highlighted.

Global Viewpoints is designed for a broad spectrum of readers who want to learn more about current events, history, political science, government, international relations, economics, environmental science, world cultures, and sociology—students doing research for class assignments or debates, teachers and faculty seeking to supplement course materials, and others wanting to understand current issues better. By presenting how people in various countries perceive the root causes, current consequences, and proposed solutions to worldwide challenges, Global Viewpoints volumes offer readers opportunities to enhance their global awareness and their knowledge of cultures worldwide.

Introduction

> "Significant medical and pharmacological discoveries are made through greater understanding of the earth's biodiversity. Loss in biodiversity may limit discovery of potential treatments for many diseases and health problems."
> —World Health Organization

Biodiversity is generally thought of as an ecological and environmental issue, but it can also be a medical one. Many medicines and curatives are derived from plant or animal sources. Thus, ecological biodiversity can have a direct benefit to human health.

Aaron S. Bernstein and David S. Ludwig discuss some of the advantages of biodiversity in a November 19, 2008, article in the *Journal of the American Medical Association*. They explain:

> Natural products compose a superb resource for drug discovery because they have evolved in some cases during millions of years, to exploit fundamental biological pathways often shared by humans. In addition, the random aspect of the evolutionary process gives rise to products with unforeseen, and perhaps unforeseeable, biological actions, allowing for the development of pharmaceuticals with novel mechanisms for action.

As an example, the authors point to a common flower, the petunia. Scientists trying to produce colored petals in petunias unexpectedly created flowers that were instead mostly or entirely white. When the scientists investigated, they discovered that the petunias possessed a mechanism for inhibiting gene expression. This mechanism has the potential to treat numerous medical conditions, including neurodegenerative disease and cancer. For their work inspired by the petunia, the scientists were awarded the Nobel Prize in 2006.

Rain forests, with their rich biodiversity, are especially important as a source for medicines. Rhett Butler in a July 22, 2012, post at Mongabay.com writes:

> The rain forest has been called the ultimate chemical laboratory with each rain forest species experimenting with various chemical defenses to ensure survival in the harsh world of natural selection.

Butler adds that rain forest plants have provided medicine for everything from childhood leukemia to toothaches, and that 70 percent of plants identified with anticancer characteristics come from the rain forest.

Butler argues that medicinal plants can be a huge source of wealth for countries in which the rain forests are located. That wealth, in turn, could be used to preserve and maintain the rain forest and its biodiversity. Unfortunately, however, the profits from medicine rarely go to the countries from which the medicine comes. Instead, companies in industrialized countries often patent the medicine themselves, even though, in some cases, the plants may have been used by indigenous doctors for generations. For example, Butler points to yagé, a hallucinogenic that has long been used by Amazonian peoples. An American entrepreneur named Loren Miller visited Ecuador in the 1980s, took some yagé, and patented it for psychiatric use. The resulting battle over the patent dragged through the 1990s, only ending when the patent expired in 2003.

Nature, then, contains a huge number of potential medicines and cures for human illnesses. Scientists and conservationists have long worried that biodiversity loss may destroy or drive into extinction medicinal species. For example, an October 17, 2003, post at ScienceDaily discussed the five hundred species of cone snails that are found in shallow tropical seas. The snails stun their prey with a mix of toxins. Each species has its own set of poisons, and the poison is constantly altered and adjusted to prevent the prey from developing resistance. Early research has suggested that the cone snail's toxins may have great potential in developing medicines for humans. For instance, one drug developed from the snail toxins is Prialt, which may be one thousand times more potent than morphine in the treatment of pain but without morphine's addictive qualities.

Unfortunately, according to Eric Chivian, a Harvard researcher quoted in the ScienceDaily article, "Wild populations [of cone snails] are being decimated by habitat destruction and overexploitation." Chivian adds, "To lose these species would be a self-destructive act of unparalleled folly." Cone snail shells are attractive and have long been collected and sold. The snails are also threatened by coastal development, fishing, and pollution. Chivian and his co-researchers worry that, with so many threats, cone snail species may be wiped out before their true value to humans can even be assessed.

If biodiversity loss can threaten potential medicines, it is also true that medicine, or reported medicinal qualities, can be a threat to biodiversity. For instance, Westerners have long incorrectly believed that the horn of a rhinoceros has aphrodisiac qualities. This is false—but now, suddenly, people in Vietnam seem to have picked up the legend and are treating it as true. In addition, many Vietnamese have become convinced that rhino horns may help cure cancer.

Though there is no real evidence for either of these claims, the rumors have made rhino horns very valuable, and more and more rhinos are being poached and killed. David Smith in a September 3, 2012, article in the *Guardian* reports that in South Africa poachers used to kill around fourteen rhinos a year. Now that number has exploded, with 333 rhinos killed in 2010 and 448 in 2011. Tom Milliken, an official with the wildlife trade-monitoring network TRAFFIC, is quoted in the *Guardian* as saying, "Losing 500 a year, when it used to be 12 or 14 a year, is a crisis." Milliken also noted, "Rhino horn is fetching the highest prices I've ever seen in my career."

Its link to medicine is but one of the ways in which biodiversity affects human well-being and is affected by human actions. *Global Viewpoints: Biodiversity* looks at these and other important relationships between humans and biodiversity in chapters titled Biodiversity and Economic Development, Biodiversity and Wildlife, Biodiversity and Agriculture, and Biodiversity and Climate Change. Writers from around the world offer different viewpoints on the importance of biodiversity for both humans and the planet.

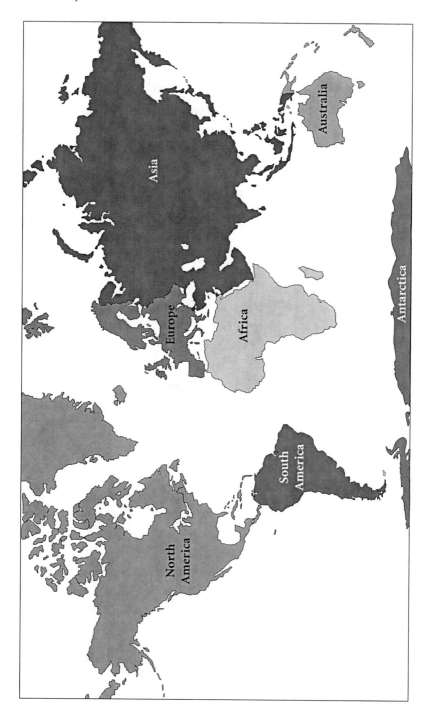

 GLOBALVIEWPOINTS

CHAPTER

Biodiversity and Economic Development

Business Must Be Given a Role in Promoting Biodiversity

James Griffiths

James Griffiths is managing director of ecosystems at the World Business Council for Sustainable Development. In the following viewpoint, he argues that businesses have a vital stake in biodiversity and ecological conservation since environmental degradation can have a major impact on investment and planning. He says, however, that business interests and input have not been sufficiently considered in plans for biodiversity conservation. He concludes that businesses need to embrace biodiversity conservation and that government planners need to work more closely with businesses in developing standards.

As you read, consider the following questions:

1. According to Griffiths, what policies and regulations can effective partnerships between business and government deliver?

2. What does Griffiths say was one of the "key findings" of the report, and what does he say needs to be reexamined?

3. What does Griffiths say will happen to ecosystems over the next forty years, and what does he say this means for business?

Business can be a significant driver of biodiversity conservation but it must have a seat at the table and be allowed to have a constructive role in designing and implementing sustainable policy solutions with governments.

A Billion People

This was at the core of messages the World Business Council for Sustainable Development (WBCSD) delivered last week [in November 2010] during the COP [Conference of the Parties] 10 Convention on Biological Diversity (CBD) in Nagoya [Japan].

Forty years from now—in 2050—we will live in a very different world in which the population will soar to 9 billion. If you consider the implications of that growth, it is no wonder that already today some businesses are making biodiversity issues a top priority in their business models and sustainability strategies.

Potential ecosystem degradation and biodiversity loss are material considerations for all investment decisions. Not because they make for good public relations, but because companies and investors realized that these are fundamental for business success in our carbon and natural resource constrained world.

Unfortunately, under the current CBD framework, business does not have a clearly defined role in the process of discussing and creating international policy solutions—and regional and national involvement is extremely variable.

International governments will not be able to create a more sustainable world on their own and harnessing business as a progressive actor and utilizing market forces to shape consumption trends will be vital ingredients to achieving the 2020 biodiversity goals set out in the CBD's new strategic plan agreed to in Nagoya.

That is why government and business will need to form partnerships to bring any serious hope of halting and reversing the current loss of biodiversity and degradation of critical ecosystems and the services they deliver. Effective partnerships can deliver environmental policies and regulations that establish a level playing field; leverage market forces; set realistic targets; are predictive, transparent, consistent and time tabled; and create appropriate incentives for sustainable use.

Businesses Can Play a Significant Role

A report released in Nagoya identifies the significant role businesses can play in achieving biodiversity conservation and sustainable use of natural resources. Entitled "Effective Biodiversity and Ecosystem Policy and Regulation," it provides the first comprehensive business response to biodiversity policy proposals highlighted by the Economics of Ecosystems and Biodiversity (TEEB) initiative that was endorsed in Nagoya.

The report's goal is to provide insights from a business perspective on public policy options that can achieve the greatest positive impact on biodiversity and ecosystem. It includes case studies from six WBCSD member companies—Natura, Rio Tinto, Fibria, Weyerhaeuser, Volkswagen and PwC [PricewaterhouseCoopers]—illustrating how companies can help address biodiversity loss and ecosystems degradation through new or adapted policy frameworks and regulatory approaches, often building on existing voluntary actions, such as standard setting and third-party certification.

> *Business must accept that change is needed, and governments must transition sectors and communities off current subsidies that undermine biodiversity objectives.*

The policy options report was supported by a companion case study library "Responding to the Biodiversity Challenge"—illustrating how a further 28 WBCSD companies already support the CBD's three core objectives of conservation, sustainable use and equitable benefit sharing through their current business practices.

These kinds of strategies will need to be scaled up, spread and incentivized to deliver real results in combating biodiversity loss. Creating policy mechanisms that leverage market forces and create economic incentives for conservation will help to drive the inclusion of biodiversity and ecosystem value in business decision making and will level the playing field between businesses who are taking their responsibilities seriously and those who are not.

One of the key findings of the report was that subsidy reform is long on rhetoric and short on action. Both governments and businesses will need to reexamine subsidy reform.

Business must accept that change is needed, and governments must transition sectors and communities off current subsidies that undermine biodiversity objectives. Transparency on existing subsidies is a precondition for a well-informed public debate on reform, and the private sector's economic and industry analysis should be called upon to help understand the dependency and impact. Market mechanisms used to address climate change and carbon emissions globally, and biodiversity and ecosystems locally (like wetland conservation), provide frameworks on which to build regional and national ecological service markets and conservation banking structures.

In addition, many of the current targets and accounting structures are simply too vague and difficult to track their accountability. It's crucial that these measurements are made relevant for business, with business assigned a clear role in their delivery. Improved green accounting will certainly help progress national approaches for valuing ecosystems and ecosystem services in economic terms, thereby making sure that public and private sector decision making around biodiversity becomes more intuitive and effective or, in economic terms, ensuring the internalization of ecosystem externalities.

Policy makers and business cannot keep doing things the same way and expect different results for biodiversity.

Change for Business and for Ecosystems

All companies affect ecosystems and are dependent on functioning ecosystems to remain in business. Over the next 40 years, ecosystems will be altered faster and more extensively than ever before—posing significant business risks as well as opportunities for new eco-efficient goods, services and technologies.

Supporting business as a solutions provider through investment incentives and policy frameworks that mitigate negative impacts and reward ecosystem stewardship and sustainable use will ensure a preferred future for us all.

Policy makers and business cannot keep doing things the same way and expect different results for biodiversity. Business can no longer ignore its biodiversity impacts and dependence—and governments must seek business input to their public policy forums.

WBCSD therefore welcomed the constructive aspiration that came out of the discussions in Nagoya to increase business engagement, especially in the redrafting of national biodiversity strategies and action plans. The business sector is looking forward to working with national governments ready to translate this aspiration into effective dialogue and real action.

Biodiversity Could Be Casualty of Myanmar Openness

Denis D. Gray

Denis D. Gray is the Associated Press Bangkok bureau chief. In the following viewpoint, he reports that the isolation of Myanmar's repressive government has helped to slow development and preserve environmental resources in the nation. Now, however, Myanmar is moving toward greater political openness. As a result, Gray says, it may see foreign investment and rapid development. This may degrade the environment, he warns, especially since the government remains corrupt and may be uninterested in protecting the environment. This concerns environmentalists since Myanmar has rich biodiversity and some of the region's greatest remaining natural resources.

As you read, consider the following questions:

1. What evidence does Gray point to in order to show that the rush is already on to exploit Myanmar's natural resources?

2. From its position at the center of an area rich in biodiversity, Myanmar has plant and animal life characteristic of which neighboring regions, according to Gray?

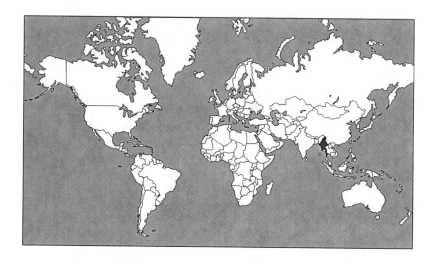

3. What does Gray say is lacking from Myanmar's fifty major hydro projects?

As many as 40,000 gorgeously plumed birds known as the Gurney's Pitta thrive in the lowland rain forests of economically backward Myanmar. Across the border, Thailand's last five pairs are guarded around the clock against snakes and human predators.

The bird's status is among many reasons Myanmar is regarded as one of Asia's last bastions of biodiversity, and why environmentalists view the country's steps toward opening its doors with some fear.

Myanmar has avoided the rapid, often rampant development seen in Thailand and other parts of Asia because of decades of isolation brought on by harsh military rule. But as foreign investors begin pouring in, activists in what was once known as Burma say endemic corruption, virtually nonexistent environmental laws and a long-repressed civil society make it "ripe for environmental rape."

They hope that it will at least prove a race: Pro-democracy reformers and conservationists are urging the government to put more safeguards in place against the unscrupulous eager to take advantage of their absence.

The rush is already on. Airplanes bound for Yangon, the nation's largest city, are booked up with businessmen looking for deals, along with throngs of tourists. Singapore dispatched a delegation with 74 company representatives in March while the Malaysians sent a high-level investment mission focused on property development, tourism, rubber and oil palm plantations. U.S. and European countries are not as involved because sanctions against Myanmar prevent them from starting new businesses there.

"The 'development invasion' will speed up environmental destruction and is also likely to lead to more human rights abuses," says Pianporn Deetes of the U.S.-based International Rivers network. "Industries will move very fast, while civil society is just beginning to learn about the impacts."

Myanmar is home to 1,099 of Southeast Asia's 1,324 bird species and to extensive coral reefs. Unexploited rivers, on- and offshore oil deposits and minerals abound.

Under President Thein Sein, the government last year began to loosen the military's grip on power, instituting some reforms and even allowing democracy leader Aung San Suu Kyi to run, and win, a seat in Parliament. Reasons for the changes remain murky, but years as an international pariah have left Myanmar poor and in need of foreign investment.

Environmentally, Myanmar is certainly no longer pristine, but it has been spared some of the wholesale ravages seen in the economically booming, more open societies across Asia.

Positioned at the core of one of the world's richest biodiversity hot spots, it's endowed with plant and animal life of the flanking Himalayas, Malay peninsula, Indian subcontinent and mainland Southeast Asia.

Only three countries in the world have more extensive tropical forests: Brazil, India and the Congo. Myanmar is home to 1,099 of Southeast Asia's 1,324 bird species and to extensive coral reefs. Unexploited rivers, on- and offshore oil deposits and minerals abound.

"The scale is just massive. It just dwarfs everything else in surrounding countries," says Robert J. Tizard, who heads the office of the New York–based Wildlife Conservation Society in Myanmar. "It could be a curse that they have so many resources."

Environmentalists say Myanmar's government, which remains dominated by the military, has an abysmal record of protecting its resources, which are often exploited by enterprises linked to generals and their cronies.

One such enterprise, the Yuzana Company, operates in the Hukaung Valley Wildlife Sanctuary, which the government established with considerable fanfare as the world's largest tiger reserve in 2001. Yuzana has razed forests in the area to plant sugar cane, and gold mining is rife.

According to spokesman Ah Nah of the Kachin Development Networking Group, which has been monitoring the valley since 2007, virtually all the concessions are within the reserve boundaries. WCS, which pushed the regime to set up the sanctuary, says only 25 percent of Yuzana's plantations are in the park.

The Myanmar company's owner, tycoon Htay Myint, enjoys close links to the military. The country's largest money-spinning industries—energy, mining and electricity—and those related to the environment are all led by retired generals.

Jonathan Eames of BirdLife International, which has been tracking the status of the Gurney's Pitta, says efforts to create a park to protect the bird's habitat failed because of the

The United States Engages Myanmar

Secretary [of State Hillary] Clinton: Well, Mr. President [Thein Sein of Myanmar], it's wonderful to see you again, as you say, for our third meeting. I believe we have had productive discussions in Naypyidaw and in Siem Reap, and I look forward to such a discussion here in New York. We have watched as you and your government have continued the steady process of reform, and we've been pleased to respond with specific steps that recognize the government's efforts and encourage further reform.

And in recognition of the continued progress toward reform and in response to requests from both the government and the opposition, the United States is taking the next step in normalizing our commercial relationship. We will begin the process of easing restrictions on imports of Burmese goods into the United States. We hope this will provide more opportunities for your people to sell their goods into our market. As we do so, we will continue consulting with Congress and other relevant stakeholders about additional steps, while at the same time working with you and supporting those who are hoping that the reform will be permanent and progress will be continuing.

We recognize, Mr. President, that you are doing many things at once—political reform, moving toward a democratic change; economic reform, moving toward greater connection of your country with the global economy; working to end ethnic conflicts as you move toward peace and stability for your country.

So I look forward to our discussion today, Mr. President. Thank you.

Hillary Rodham Clinton and Thein Sein,
"Clinton's Remarks with Burmese President Thein Sein,
September 2012," Council on Foreign Relations, September 26, 2012.

military's push to replace forests with oil palm plantations in the Tenasserim Range. Similar clearing occurred earlier across the bird's territory in Thailand.

Myanmar operators proved less than competent so deforestation has slowed, but Eames expects it to accelerate again as Malaysians, Indonesians and Thais, experts at plantation management, move in.

Foreign enterprises already have taken advantage elsewhere. Thai companies, particularly in the 1990s, decimated teak forests in eastern Myanmar and are poised to become major players at Dawei, a deep sea port and vast industrial estate being built by Thailand's largest construction enterprise, Italian-Thai Development. It has recently drawn protests by locals fearing pollution of what is now an unsullied region.

Pianporn says a number of Thai companies, faced with increasingly tougher environmental laws at home, are planning to relocate their "dirty industries," including petrochemical and coal-fired plants, next door.

A surge in hydroelectric projects is also expected, with China, the no. 1 investor in Myanmar, leading the charge. In face of strong domestic protests, the regime last September suspended construction of the Myitsone dam on the Irrawaddy River although environmental groups recently report that work by the China Power Investment company quietly continues around the dam site.

Chinese loggers have stripped large areas of northern Kachin State and others threaten southern regions.

Activists stress that environmentally harmful projects often go hand in hand with human rights abuses such as forced labor and mass relocations.

Myanmar officials say they are not blind to the dangers.

Ko Ko Hlaing, an adviser to the president, said bids by foreign investors will be scrutinized to ensure they adhere to a policy of sustainable development.

"We Myanmar citizens are quite aware of the consequences. We cannot allow our cherished motherland to be destroyed by greedy foreign investors," he said in a statement to the Associated Press.

In his inaugural address, Thein Sein pledged "serious attention" to protecting forests and wildlife, reducing air and water pollution and controlling dumping of industrial waste.

But the good intentions could be dashed given Myanmar's vulnerabilities.

The country ranked 180 out of 183 countries on global transparency's 2011 corruption index and is only now debating an environmental law in Parliament. Only sketchy guidelines for sustainable development exist.

None of the some 50 major hydro projects completed, under construction or on the drawing boards are known to have any environmental impact statements that would meet international standards, according to International Rivers network and other environmental watchdogs.

The Ministry of Environment Conservation and Forestry was formed only last year and is still without a conservation division. Tizard, who works closely with the ministry, says it has some officials who are dedicated to their work, but he and other environmentalists note that their efforts can be easily subverted.

"Under-the-table deals are likely to continue because the military is so entrenched. They or their cronies control most of the businesses while civil society is still very weak. It needs a lot of education," says Wong Aung, of the Burma Environmental Working Group, a network of 10 grassroots organizations.

"It's a double-edged sword. There will be economic development and you are going to have trade-offs with the environment," says Robert Mather, head of the IUCN, International Union for Conservation of Nature, in Southeast Asia.

There are, he says, some grounds for optimism.

Myanmar has a conservation tradition, including sound forestry practices that are lacking in many surrounding countries, and it appears eager to seek outside assistance. A number of international environmental organizations are already planning to set up there, some in partnership with the growing number of local groups. The Wildlife Conservation Society is currently the only major one with a permanent presence.

"You are going back to Thailand in the 1950s with conservation practices of the 21st century, so there is a lot of opportunity to do it right."

Mather says Myanmar, as "the last frontier," could play hard to get—picking only those investors with a history of transparency and environmental sensitivity.

The selection would expand greatly if economic sanctions by Western nations were lifted. The European Union announced last month it will suspend most sanctions for a year while it assesses the country's progress toward democracy, while the United States is taking a wait-and-see attitude.

"You are going back to Thailand in the 1950s with conservation practices of the 21st century, so there is a lot of opportunity to do it right," Tizard says. "If they follow some of the best practices they could do incredibly well."

Development and Political Conflict Threaten Palestine's Plant Biodiversity

Roubina Basous Ghattas

Roubina Basous Ghattas is the biodiversity specialist at the Applied Research Institute–Jerusalem (ARIJ). In the following viewpoint, she says that the Palestinian territories have traditionally been home to a wide range of biodiversity, including a plethora of plant life. However, in recent years plant life in the territories has been declining rapidly. She says this is caused by development, habitat destruction, and political turmoil with Israel that has resulted in habitats being divided and sectioned off. She says that the territories and international groups should move quickly to try to conserve remaining plant life and prevent further degradation.

As you read, consider the following questions:

1. What life-sustaining crops does Ghattas say originated in Palestine?

2. How many species do experts say require urgent conservation measures, and what does Ghattas say will happen if these are not forthcoming?

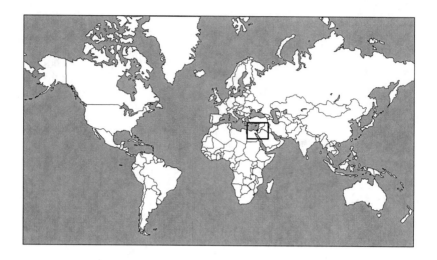

3. What was found when ARIJ looked at floral surveys in the Palestinian territories over the last twenty to forty years?

Biodiversity encompasses all biological entities that occur as an interacting system in a habitat or ecosystem, and plants constitute a very important segment of such biological systems. Plant biodiversity is an irreplaceable resource, providing raw materials for introduction and domestication as well as improvement programmes in agriculture and forestry.

The Fertile Crescent

Palestine is a treasure chest of biodiversity that hosts a large variety of plants. As part of the Fertile Crescent, it has been identified as an important centre of genetic diversity for the life-sustaining crops of wheat, barley, vines, olives, onions, and pulses, which all originated within the geographical land of Palestine. Palestinians have used these natural resources to respond to various needs in their lives. It is worth adding that Palestine is characterized by its unique variable ecosystems that encounter various floral associations. This location also nurtures Palestinian biological diversity, through which climatic zones, desert, steppe, Mediterranean woodland, and even oases join one another in this compact geographical area.

Despite its small size, the Palestinian territory (PT) comprises approximately 3 percent of the global biodiversity and contains a high density of species and a large number of endemic species (endemics are only found in restricted regions and therefore harbour unique genetic information), reaching up to 5 percent (120 endemics) of the total number of plants that grow in PT, such as caper, Palestinian sea blite, majoram, iris, fluellen and others. It is also known for its unique forested areas, which comprise 4.45 percent of the total area of PT.

The sustainability of its natural and human systems is not only threatened endogenously—i.e., by the development process from within—but it is also impeded exogenously by the political conflict it faces.

According to a recent survey done by a specialized ARIJ (Applied Research Institute–Jerusalem) team in the year 2006, it was found that 2,076 plant species inhabit the West Bank and Gaza Strip alone (75.5 percent of species in Mandate of Palestine), where 1,959 species in 115 families are growing in the West Bank and 1,290 species in 105 families are growing in the Gaza Strip, of which 117 species grow only in the Gaza Strip. These numbers were ascertained during a comprehensive study to assess the status of flora only in the geographical area of the West Bank and Gaza Strip.

PT's landscape of flowers and plants changes abruptly with its various geographical regions. The richness of the flora as a whole is partly explained by the uniqueness of the Palestinian climate, which appears to favour great regional variations in plants. . . .

Plant Decline

However, the plant genetic resources of PT have been declining constantly over the years. The Palestinian context offers a unique case where the sustainability of its natural and human systems is not only threatened endogenously—i.e., by the development process from within—but it is also impeded exogenously by the political conflict it faces. The landscape, ecosystems, and vegetation of PT, in particular, have been subjected to changes on a large scale. The rate of natural destruction in PT is much higher nowadays with the appearance of new challenges that face biodiversity. Habitat destruction comes from a broad range of sources that include unplanned urban expansion; overgrazing; overexploitation; deforestation and unplanned forestry activities; desertification and drought; invasive alien species; and pollution and contaminants, in addition to the political status, which includes the division of Palestinian accessible areas, land confiscation, and fragmentation of habitats mainly as a result of the segregation wall [the Israeli West Bank barrier built inside the West Bank by Israel in violation of an ICJ (International Court of Justice) July 9, 2009, opinion]. These factors all serve to affect genetic exchange and, as a result, will weaken species composition in the future, thus precipitating the loss of this valuable heritage.

These problems are causing drastic changes and have left deep traces on the landscape, the natural resources, and the natural vegetation of the area.

Of the surveyed 2,076 plant species that grow in the West Bank and Gaza, 636 are listed as endangered, of which 90 species are very rare. It is also contended by experts that urgent conservation measures are required for more than 40 species. As a result, it is predicted that in Palestine, a number of species will disappear within the next ten years unless urgent measures are taken to protect, preserve, and develop their utilization.

A comparison between the floral surveys over the past 20 to 40 years was done by a specialized ARIJ team, where it was found that 370 species have changed their status and become rare or very rare in the West Bank and Gaza during the last 30 years. Such results indicate that the plant species growing in PT are subjected to pressures of various types, which cause a reduction in number and dramatically threaten their existence. Thus, if the root causes for such changes are going to continue, the existence of those species and others is threatened with unsustainability and lack of viability for the long run.

Drastic Changes

These problems are causing drastic changes and have left deep traces on the landscape, the natural resources, and the natural vegetation of the area. At the moment, there is hardly any natural, undisturbed vegetation in the area. In addition, such pressure on the integrity of ecosystems and stability of natural resources increases the risk of losing the livelihood as well as the historical, cultural, environmental, and economic value of Palestinian biodiversity, despite the fact that these costs are difficult to quantify, or may indeed be immeasurable and irreplaceable.

In conclusion, the continued pressures on the Palestinian indigenous plants will inevitably impair the rights of future generations if sustainable utilization measures are not implemented. As a long-term research endeavour, it is necessary to increase Palestinian knowledge concerning how human and natural systems interact; whereas in the short run, approaches for monitoring and forecasting human impacts on Palestinian ecosystems must be developed. Criteria and indicators for social, economic, and biological components of plant ecosystems are the core of current sustainability initiatives. This is in addition to biodiversity conservation and better management, legislation and regulation, public awareness and training, research, protection of intellectual property rights, gender role, indigenous knowledge, improvement of ecotourism, local institutional co-operation, international and regional co-operation and coordination, and improvement of livelihood and community development—all important issues to be tackled in order to reach a state where the utilization and conservation of the Palestinian biological resources are well shared and protected within Palestinian society.

The Development of Tourism Is Destroying Biodiversity on the Galápagos Islands

Carole Cadwalladr

Carole Cadwalladr is a British author as well as a columnist and features writer at the Observer. *In the following viewpoint, she reports on the rapid growth of development and tourism in the Galápagos Islands. She says that this development is harming the wildlife and plant life for which the Galápagos Islands are known. For instance, cars and planes kill thousands of birds and lizards each year, and tourists bring invasive plant and animal species with them that overrun the islands and force out native species. Cadwalladr says that if action is not taken quickly, the rich biodiversity of the Galápagos Islands will be irreparably destroyed.*

As you read, consider the following questions:

1. According to Cadwalladr, how did finches on the Galápagos Islands help Charles Darwin with his theory of evolution?

2. What are some of the art projects at the Bluecoat arts center in Liverpool that were inspired by the islands, as Cadwalladr describes?

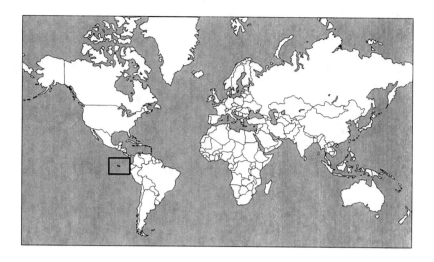

3. Why was the sewage plant on Isabela Island ineffective, according to the viewpoint?

Opening what looks like the drawer of an office filing cabinet, Gustavo Jiménez[-Uzcátegui], a scientist at the Charles Darwin Foundation on the Galápagos, reaches inside, rummages around for a bit, and then pulls out not a report or a file, but a massive stuffed albatross. It's about the size of a toddler, just one of hundreds of stuffed birds and animals in the foundation's vertebrate collection.

Development and Extinction

We have already seen a stuffed Baltra Island iguana, a 4ft-long, scaly, dragon-like creature that was successfully brought back from near extinction in the 1930s, but has the misfortune to live on one of the two islands that have an airport. About once a month, Jiménez[-Uzcátegui] receives a body that has been flattened by a bus or landed on by an aircraft.

Then there are the finches, the songbirds that inspired Charles Darwin to formulate the theory of evolution. It was the differing length of their beaks that helped lead him to the notion that they had evolved differently according to their environment. Now they are roadkill. "There are now so many people living in the highlands," says Jiménez[-Uzcátegui]. "So many cars. It's impossible to estimate how many are run over a year, but at least 10,000." To put this in context, there are only just over 100 left of the most endangered type, the mangrove finch.

In the filing cabinets of life on these islands, the waved albatross—the only albatross to live in the tropics—is just another Galápagan hard-luck story: Regularly caught up in fishing nets, it's on the critically endangered species list with a "high risk of extinction in the wild".

The collection is supposed to be a catalogue of life, but increasingly it looks more like one of death. Of species threatened. Disappearing. Missing. Of an entire ecosystem under threat. Because there is nowhere quite like the Galápagos. In every sense. For its profound isolation in the Pacific Ocean, its unique biodiversity—home to hundreds of endemic species—and for its pristine, untouched environment.

"If you look at graphs of tourism and invasive species, they go absolutely together."

Except, as even a glance around the harbour of Puerto Ayora, the main town on the island of Santa Cruz, will show you, it's no longer pristine. A filmy slick of oil shines on the surface of the water where hundreds of boats wait to receive the next intake of tourists. And beyond is a large town, a mess of shanty suburbs and half-finished hotels. The groundwater is contaminated and there's no proper sewerage. Dozens and dozens of Toyota pickups wait to ferry the tourists around.

What many people don't realise is that the Galápagos, as well as being one of the most fragile environments on earth, is also one of the fastest-growing economies in South America. Per capita income is higher here than anywhere else in Ecuador. Nearly 40,000 people have made their home here, drawn by tourism, and with them have come hundreds of introduced species, invasive plants and an infrastructure that simply can't cope.

Paradise in Crisis

For anyone who grew up watching David Attenborough and giant tortoises on *Life on Earth* [a BBC natural history television series originally broadcast in 1979], it's a shock. This isn't what Charles Darwin's earthly paradise is meant to look like, although Noémi d'Ozouville, an earth scientist who lives in Puerto Ayora and studies freshwater dynamics, sighs when I say this. "That's the thing with the stories about the Galápagos: it's either paradise or paradise in crisis."

The problem with this is that it is in crisis. In the bowels of the Charles Darwin Foundation, Henri Herrera, an entomologist, pulls out drawers of preserved ants. They're his specialist field—he points out that Darwin studied them too—but new types of ants keep arriving all the time. In aircraft, on boats, in the bags of tourists, in cargo shipments. "I sampled two boats and found 600 different species of insects in my traps. If you look at graphs of tourism and invasive species, they go absolutely together."

It's not difficult to understand the threat. He pulls out a drawer of native endemic ants and then a recent introduction, a bigheaded ant. It's not just its head that is bigger. "The thing is that invertebrates are crucial to the ecosystem. If you destroy them, you destroy the ecosystem; it's at the base of it all."

It's this conflict between man and nature that's at the heart of a new exhibition on the Galápagos at the Bluecoat arts centre in Liverpool [United Kingdom]. It's the result of an initiative by the [Calouste] Gulbenkian Foundation and the Galápagos Conservation Trust. Over a period of four years, they have sent 11 artists to the islands and the exhibition features works as diverse as photographs of cockfighting by Jeremy Deller, the sound of sharks underwater by Kaffe Matthews and, most arrestingly of all, footage of Marcus Coates dressed up as a bird, in a cardboard box, with a cardboard beak and cardboard wings, wandering the streets of Puerto Ayora.

"There's constantly more, more, more. More flights, more hotels, more cars. It's uncontrolled."

Four years on, he's still vividly remembered. Enrique Ramos, owner and editor of the Galápagos newspaper *El Colono*, said it had been a startling moment. Coates had dressed up as a booby—the blue-footed bird that inhabits the islands—and received an amazed reaction from residents. "It was a kind of communication that was totally new for us. To dress up like this. As a way of expressing feelings. People hadn't seen that before."

But the shock worked both ways. "I had no idea that anyone even lived on the Galápagos," says Coates. "There's this huge conflict between people and animals and this bizarre situation where people are almost second-class citizens compared to the wildlife." The impact on his art has been profound, he says; it's made him entirely rethink what it is to be human.

Coates's work explored the interaction of animals and people, but what's abundantly clear if you spend any time at all on the Galápagos is that the needs of human habitation and the needs of preserving a pristine environment are incompatible.

People vs. Wildlife

"It's unsustainable," says Felipe Cruz, the director of technical assistance at the Charles Darwin Foundation. "There's constantly more, more, more. More flights, more hotels, more cars. It's uncontrolled. We talk about ecotourism but in reality it's already showing signs of being mass tourism. People aren't even coming for the wildlife anymore. They just come for a vacation."

Everywhere there are signs of stress. On Isabela Island, Maximilian Martin takes us on a tour of the rubbish dump where feral cats roam and of a defunct sewerage plant. "An international organisation spent something like £485,000 on it, but the local people didn't know how to use it. So now the waste is just going into the ground untreated. Technically, the problems are solved. The expertise is here. The problem is social."

Martin works for the WWF [World Wildlife Fund] conservation group and Isabela now has a successful recycling programme. It's not that efforts aren't being made to address the problem, just that the scale of it is so enormous. Mile upon mile of the countryside around Puerto Villamil, Isabela's main town, has been smothered by an invasive creeper. On Santa Cruz, a type of blackberry, impossible to remove, has overrun the highlands, destroying vast tracts of habitat.

Yet it is still an extraordinary place. Even in Isabela's port, among the boats and the noise, there are penguins and stingrays and pelicans and when I go for a swim, I end up frolicking with a group of sea lions that behave more like a litter of puppies. At one point, one of them swims away and returns with a stick.

It's heartbreaking to see what is happening to the islands. Dorothy Cross, an Irish artist who participated in the programme, had visited the Galápagos 12 years previously, and was shocked by how much it had changed. "I really felt disquiet. Being there felt like a very difficult predicament. I live in nature and a lot of my work is rooted in nature and in the Galápagos this extraordinariness is being undermined by tourism and money."

All of the artists returned, says Cross, "a bit disheartened and anxious". As a tourist, whisked off on a boat, you do not necessarily see the towns and one of the key ideas behind the scheme was to provide people with another view of the islands. Robert Silbermann, the chief executive of the Galápagos Conservation Trust, says that sending the artists to the islands was intended to give people a different angle on the place. "If you look at some of the work, cockfighting and unfinished houses and buildings, these are not the usual images of the Galápagos that you see.

"What's clear," he adds, "is that things have to change. Things can't continue in the way they have been. There is a need to take action now. It can't wait five years".

"Because if we can't save Galápagos, then we can't save anywhere."

Time Running Out

But what action? Art will not save the Galápagos, but maybe it can provide a sense of urgency. It's not clear what else will. In a long interview, Godfrey Merlen, a British biologist who came to the islands in the early 1970s and never left, tries to remain positive, but admits he struggles. He studies the Vermilion Flycatcher, a bird that was abundant when he arrived, which is now, on the inhabited islands, vanishing before his eyes.

When Merlen first came, inspired by the environmental message of Rachel Carson's *Silent Spring* [a 1962 ecological classic], the occasional supply ship was the only way in and the only means of communication was a single radio. The isolation that made the Galápagos unique is no more. In Puerto Ayora, schoolchildren hang out in the port checking their emails and South America's newly rich pop over for a weekend minibreak.

The lives and livelihoods of 40,000 people can't be ignored, but according to Merlen, the Galápagos are the world's

Petri dish. They have to be saved. "Because if we can't save Galápagos, then we can't save anywhere."

Periodical and Internet Sources Bibliography

The following articles have been selected to supplement the diverse views presented in this chapter.

Tanya Abdallah and Khaled Swaileh — "Effects of the Israeli Segregation Wall on Biodiversity and Environmental Sustainable Development in the West Bank, Palestine," *International Journal of Environmental Studies*, vol. 68, no. 4, August 2011.

Toni Darton — "The Galapagos Islands Remain Under Threat," *Telegraph*, August 7, 2010.

Rebecca English — "Charles Plans 1,000 Eco-Houses on the Galapagos Islands After Call for Royal Help from Conservationists," *Daily Mail Online*, September 14, 2011.

Pascal Kwesiga and Sampaul Nakhaima — "Uganda: Oil—Experts Warn of Environmental Crisis," allAfrica, June 15, 2012.

Palestine Wildlife Society — "Palestine Biodiversity," January 19, 2011. http://www.wildlife-pal.org/Biodiversity.htm.

Margaret Southern — "Costa Rica: In Costa Rica There's Strength in Numbers," Nature Conservancy, February 8, 2011.

Nay Pyi Taw — "China, India, and Myanmar Design Collaboration for Sustainable Development in the Brahmaputra-Salween Landscape," ICIMOD, December 27, 2011. http://www.icimod.org/?q=6233.

UPI.com — "U.N.: Wetlands a Vital Global Resource," October 18, 2012. http://www.upi.com/Science_News/2012/10/18/UN-Wetlands-a-vital-global-resource/UPI-37131350599487.

GLOBALVIEWPOINTS

CHAPTER 2

Biodiversity and Wildlife

In Africa, Locals Must Be Involved in Balancing Hunting and Biodiversity

Kate Lee

Kate Lee is senior coordinator for sustainable markets at the International Institute for Environment and Development. In the following viewpoint, she says that balancing hunting with biodiversity is controversial. Many people argue that sanctioned hunting cannot be balanced with wildlife conservation. Lee says that, for this reason, in the past conservation efforts often focused on preserving large swathes of territory as fortresses of nature from which local peoples would be removed. However, she says that this tactic provoked resistance and was not politically sustainable. Instead, she argues, local people must be involved in conservation efforts if they are to succeed. Thus, hunting may be a part of a sustainable, inclusive conservation strategy.

As you read, consider the following questions:

1. According to Lee, to be sustainable, what should be the basis for contemporary hunting operations?
2. What do critics of CAMPFIRE say are problems with its program?

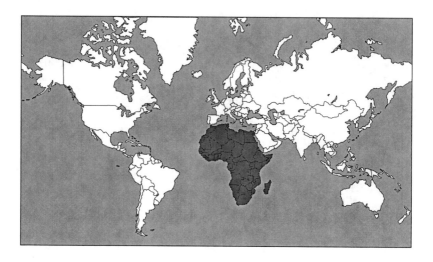

3. What was the focus of preservationist thought in the twentieth century, and why does Lee say that this was problematic?

It's a politically and ethically charged debate. Can hunting animals really contribute to wildlife conservation and biodiversity objectives? On first glance, hunting as a means of conservation seems like an inherent contradiction. Yet the sustainable use of wildlife has been ratified by the Convention on Biological Diversity (CBD) as a central means of conserving biodiversity. So is hunting sustainable and does it actually incentivise conservation? And is it really the right way to sustain biodiversity?

The Argument Against Hunting

Many feel hunting is unethical, is not biologically sustainable, and that the use of markets as a conservation tool will exacerbate the overuse of animals rather than conserve them. To be sustainable, low-quota selective hunting—that is, targeting older males or specific problem animals (those that kill livestock or trample crops, for example)—should be the basis for most contemporary hunting operations.

But there is a concern that hunting will be poorly controlled, and therefore unsustainable. Indiscriminate hunting of large numbers of wildlife will have a negative impact on species populations, particularly if reproductive females or young males are targeted. Social behaviour is widely observed in larger mammals and will be altered if the population and gender profile in herds are changed.

Critics suggest that scientific measurements of population numbers often do not occur, thus quotas set are unreliable and are estimates at best. Monitoring population numbers is also time consuming and expensive, and it is often difficult to estimate a particular animal's age.

One striking argument that the pro-hunting lobby presents is the role hunting can play in generating much-needed revenue for community-driven conservation initiatives.

Furthermore, sustainable hunting relies on the assumption that the quota levels set will be adhered to. This is difficult to enforce, particularly when large sums of money are involved (£50,000 plus for a lion).

Trophy hunting is surrounded by secrecy—partly because of the lack of data available but also due to the negative press it receives. More transparency and openness is needed in the industry to ensure quota levels are monitored and adhered to and population numbers can be tracked and kept stable. Any money made must be reinvested into these monitoring activities.

Nature Pays, So It Stays?

As noted, large sums of money are involved in hunting—often more so than non-extractive forms of tourism, such as photo safaris. Areas used for hunting often exceed national park di-

Economic Benefits of Hunting

In southern African countries like Zimbabwe and Namibia, the use of private and communal land areas for recreational hunting has doubled the areas under conservation management without the burden of the costs of this extra management falling on to already stretched state conservation agencies. In turn, the use of such lands for recreational hunting can provide community benefits in remote rural areas.

Proponents also claim that the high financial returns derived from recreational hunting can provide important benefits to national exchequers and to local communities. The daily rates charged to recreational hunters who travel as tourists to developing countries are much higher per capita than are those generally charged for game-viewing tourism. Furthermore, hunting and trophy fees are set at hundreds and thousands of dollars per trophy, depending on the species killed, while park entrance fees are set in fives, tens and twenties of dollars. Therefore, game-viewing tourists need to be accommodated in much larger numbers than do hunters to achieve the same returns. In turn, recreational hunters have much lower infrastructural requirements than game-viewing tourists who may have considerable direct environmental impacts, for example through their need for lodges and roads, and for water extraction and waste disposal.

Nigel Leader-Williams, "Conservation and Hunting: Friends or Foes?," Recreational Hunting, Conservation, and Rural Livelihoods: Science and Practice. *Eds. Barney Dickson, Jonathan Hutton, and Bill Adams. Hoboken, NJ: Blackwell, 2009.*

mensions so economic incentives for conservation can also occur over far greater areas of land than through photo tourism, which is often confined within national park boundaries.

One striking argument that the pro-hunting lobby presents is the role hunting can play in generating much-needed revenue for community-driven conservation initiatives. One of the most well-known community-managed programmes is CAMPFIRE (Communal Areas Management Programme for Indigenous Resources) in Zimbabwe. Revenues from hunting have helped change attitudes towards wildlife in local communities and have resulted in more land being turned over to wildlife management projects. Poaching levels can also decrease as community-managed monitoring is more active.

The support of . . . local people who inhabit the same areas as wildlife is essential.

But even community-based methods of wildlife management have their weaknesses. Critics of CAMPFIRE argue that it focuses too much on financial incentives and the commodification of wildlife and not enough on the importance of biodiversity conservation. The process of making money becomes the end in itself. Money can also end up in the hands of a small number of elite rather than the wider community. This is often attributed to poor legislation surrounding community involvement in the industry, a lack of skills within communities to manage areas and negotiate with operators, and a failure to successfully devolve wildlife ownership to communities so they have the access and rights (and therefore ability and incentive) to manage it.

Many of the issues noted above are not associated with hunting as a conservation tool per se but with the wider political and institutional contexts in which hunting occurs. Like any conservation strategy, good governance is clearly key to successful conservation through hunting, alongside an effective and consistent population monitoring system.

People Matter

At the heart of this argument lies a fundamental difference in the perception of conservation. Preservationist thought throughout the twentieth century led to the establishment of national parks in Africa where wildlife was the only image to be seen. Protected areas or 'fortress conservation' zones were associated with the protection of nature and wildlife, and not of human populations. So historically, strategies have removed people from the land—an approach that has met resistance from local people.

There has been a move away from the preservation of wilderness ideology towards a community-centred discourse of conservation, which stresses the importance of local decision making in natural resource management. In principle, community-based conservation acknowledges that for the effective conservation of species, people living in the same area must be involved and have the legal rights and responsibilities to manage resources.

Biodiversity is intrinsically linked to the human institutions that surround it as people often depend upon biodiversity for their livelihoods. Successful biodiversity conservation depends as much on the relations between resources and its users as it does on sound scientific and biological knowledge. Hunting can conserve African wildlife effectively given the right geography and political circumstances, as it offers large financial incentives. It is also able to incentivise the conservation of particular species and the wider habitat in which they exist. This has positive spillovers for other species and the wider ecosystem. Nevertheless the support of, and devolution of control to, local people who inhabit the same areas as wildlife is essential. The long-term survival of species and their habitats will only occur if local people are deriving equitable economic and social benefits from conservation and have control over, and the right to manage, wildlife resources.

In Canada, Deer Overpopulation Threatens Biodiversity

Peter Arcese and Tara Martin

Peter Arcese is a professor and the Forest Renewal British Columbia chair in Conservation Biology, and Tara Martin is an adjunct professor, both at the University of British Columbia. In the following viewpoint, they argue that humans have eliminated many large predators, such as wolves and bobcats, in British Columbia. As a result, black-tailed deer populations have exploded. The deer, the authors say, consume edible plants, often pushing the plants to extinction. This, in turn, may destroy songbird species that rely on the plants. Despite popular resistance to the idea, the authors suggest that hunting is the best way to reduce deer populations and preserve British Columbia's biodiversity.

As you read, consider the following questions:

1. What is one familiar example of alien species introduction, according to the authors?

2. Why do the authors conclude that in the past deer probably experienced periodic extinctions from some areas in the Southern Gulf Islands?

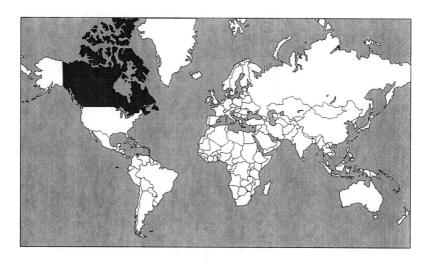

3. Why was the dark-eyed junco the only bird to be more abundant on islands with abundant deer, according to the authors?

It is well known that humans influence plant and animal species and communities directly by converting 'natural' habitats to human use. Academic researchers have spent decades documenting these changes and developing strategies to conserve valued species, including many rare mammals, plants, butterflies and birds. More recently, researchers have identified often severe, indirect effects of humans on valued native species, including those arising as a consequence of alien species introductions[1] [that is, of species to regions where they are not native], and those arising when humans facilitate the population growth of species that depredate or displace other valued species[2,3]. A familiar example in the first instance involves the introduction of the mosquito to Hawaii, which has contributed to the extinction of 28 species of Hawaiian birds thus far. Familiar examples in the second instance involve the rise of urban and rural populations of raccoons, opossums, skunks, coyotes and red foxes, which can decimate some bird, reptile and small mammal populations when abundant.

Deer Explosion

Population increases of small-bodied predators often occur when humans eliminate large-bodied predators from the landscape, because large predators like wolves, cougars and bears prey on small predators, and by doing so limit their population size. The removal of large-bodied predators by humans has also resulted in the 'release' of deer populations throughout much of North America, most notably of white-tailed deer in southern Ontario and the US, where this species has caused up to 50% declines in the number of plant species present in forests monitored over the last half century[2]. As a consequence, academics and wildlife managers now recognize that high deer densities threaten the persistence of many palatable plant species, including many iconic species of the coastal Douglas fir and Garry oak ecosystems of southeastern British Columbia[2,4,5]. Recent research in the Southern Gulf Islands of British Columbia further indicates that deer-induced changes in plant species abundance, community composition and the architecture of common palatable shrubs can profoundly affect native bird species that use understory plant species as feeding or nesting sites[5,6]. The purpose of this [viewpoint] is to very briefly summarize these effects, and to encourage local communities to consider engaging in stewardship activities to reduce the chance of plant and bird species extinctions, and to promote the recovery and diversity of native plant and bird communities in British Columbia's most threatened ecosystems[3].

Black-Tailed Deer in the Southern Gulf Islands

Black-tailed deer are endemic to the Southern Gulf Islands, as are wolves, cougars and bears. However, by the late 1800s, Europeans had removed large predators from the region[8] and became the main agent of population control for deer via hunting, until at least the late 1970s. More recently, human hunting pressure has declined or been eliminated due to increased regulation and changing human sentiment, leading to the rapid growth of deer populations and their high abundance on many islands[4,5,8]. In addition to being less dense, historic deer populations are likely to also have experienced periodic extinctions, because wolves easily eliminate deer from smaller islands which are not always readily re-colonized thereafter[8,9]. For example, although deer do swim, Ruxton Island has remained free of deer for 15 years despite lying within 1 km of DeCourcy Island, which supports a resident deer herd. Larger islands have also remained deer free for at least 35 years (e.g., Portland, Russell and Moresby Islands) despite their proximity to high-density deer populations (e.g., Salt Spring and Pender Islands). Taken together, these and other observations strongly suggest that browsing by deer on many Gulf Islands was discontinuous in time and low on average prior to the last 2–3 decades. More recently, the rapid growth of deer populations, obvious signs of browsing and extirpation of many palatable spring ephemeral plants from some islands have led to concern about the long-term effects of unregulated deer populations on the viability of many plant species[4], and on the abundance of island songbird populations which rely on understory plants for feeding and nesting[5,6].

Recent research indicates that at moderate to high densities deer have the capacity to prevent the growth of several species of meadow plants known to have been abundant historically[4], including iconic species such as common and great camas, fawn and chocolate lilies, sea blush, blue-eyed Mary, lupine, onions and various brodea. . . . On many Gulf Islands where livestock grazing and deer both occur, many palatable spring ephemerals have been extirpated, or in some cases persist as tiny grasslike individuals unable to escape predation by deer even after the removal of domestic livestock such as sheep, goats and cattle[4].

Related research also shows that deer have similar suppressive effects on many palatable species of shrubs, and that these effects in turn influence the abundance of many native songbirds[5]. . . . On Breakwater Island, for example, where deer were scarce prior to the 1980s but are now abundant, approximately 30% of ocean spray shrubs are present as dead stems only. These ghosts of past ecosystems, where spring ephemerals were common 30 years ago but are now absent, also give us a lens into the future ecosystems of islands with persistent, high-density deer populations.

In rural areas, qualified hunters operating from tree stands offer an effective and safe means of limiting deer populations.

Due to the close links between plant community composition, foliage volume and bird species abundance, researchers have also demonstrated dramatic effects of browsing on bird species abundance and diversity throughout North America[2,6], and most recently in the Southern Gulf Islands[5]. For example, in an extensive survey of 18 Gulf and San Juan Islands with different deer densities, [TG] Martin et al.[5] showed that many species that rely on understory shrubs for feeding and nesting were much less abundant on islands with high deer densities as compared to those with few or no deer. Examples include Rufous hummingbirds (9 times more abundant on islands with few versus many deer); song sparrows (4 times more abundant); yellow warblers (5 times more abundant); varied thrush (29 times more abundant); orange-crowned warblers (3.5 times more abundant); spotted towhee (25 times more abundant) and fox sparrows (9 times more abundant). Only one species, the dark-eyed junco, was significantly more abundant on islands with abundant deer, because juncos prefer open forests with little vegetative cover. As a consequence of these differences in bird species abundance, it is relatively easy for a trained observer to estimate deer density approximately in the Southern Gulf Islands by recording the frequency and diversity of bird songs.

The Future of Plant and Bird Communities of the Southern Gulf Islands and Coastal Douglas Fir Zone

Many species of birds and plants common throughout the Pacific Northwest and still abundant in many mainland and Vancouver Island habitats are now rare or absent on smaller Gulf and San Juan Islands with moderate to high deer densities, and in many forests, woodlands and meadows on larger islands. The results above, plus those from the Queen Charlotte Islands where black-tailed deer are introduced[6], further indicate that the progressive loss of understory plant species will continue where deer populations remain unregulated by large predators or human activities, leading to the extirpation of at least some bird and plant species from individual Gulf Islands. Indeed, personal stories of the decline and extirpation of the most showy and palatable plant species are already common among islanders familiar with plant identification and 20–30 years of experience observing change on their own and other properties. Comparisons of island plant communities with few deer present in the 1970s but abundant deer populations today (e.g., Breakwater Island, Piers Island) also confirm that the extirpation of common spring ephemerals can occur in as few as 30 years and indicates that widespread and still common shrub species such as ocean spray, mock orange, orange honeysuckle and flowering currant may also disappear as existing plants senesce. The absence of new arbutus recruits in moderate to heavily browsed forests is also a common observation of long-term islanders, which further suggests that a slow process of 'biotic homogenization', wherein all plant communities converge on a common template of unpalatable species, is now under way on many islands.

As palatable plant species decline, it is inevitable that birds, insect pollinators and other species not yet studied in detail will also decline, further simplifying our natural communities and reducing the natural values that draw many humans to the Southern Gulf and San Juan Islands. These changes are not the result of 'natural' processes; they are an indirect effect of the human removal of large predators, leading to the release of deer populations, and the decline of palatable plant species and the birds that depend on them. Failing to act to reduce deer populations on islands where historically abundant species are currently declining or extirpated is a decision to favour one species, the black-tailed deer, over many others that are also native to our region and valued by many humans. Ultimately, failing to reduce overabundant deer populations may also add new species to federal and provincial threatened species lists.

Options for Controlling Deer Populations

Options for controlling deer populations are widely discussed in the popular and scientific literature (e.g., see [3, 10, 11] and references therein), but highly controversial due to strong sentiments around the ethics of hunting. Because fertility control is advocated in a relatively limited set of circumstances and may require years to achieve modest reductions in population size[10], hunting remains the most effective and widely practiced method, including in many suburban areas of the Midwest US. In rural areas, qualified hunters operating from tree stands offer an effective and safe means of limiting deer populations. On smaller Gulf Islands, limiting deer densities to <0.1/km is likely to allow the persistence of most palatable plants and shrubs and may only require the removal of a few deer annually. Alternatively, investing in fertility control or animal relocation will require government approval and the willingness of communities or government agencies to fund and carry out the work. We encourage communities to consider all options as they develop local stewardship plans to conserve and restore native ecosystems.

References

1. http://www.goert.ca/about_invasive_species.php
2. http://www.actionbioscience.org/biodiversity/rooney.html#educator
3. http://www.biodiversitybc.org/EN/main/where/132.html
4. Gonzales, E.K. and P. Arcese. 2008. Herbivory, more than competition, limits early and established life stages of native plants in an invaded oak meadow. Ecology 89, 3282–3289.
5. Martin, TG., Arcese, P. and Scheerder, N. 2011. Browsing down our natural heritage: Deer impacts on vegetation structure and songbird populations across an island archipelago. Biological Conservation, in press.
6. Allombert, S., Gaston, A.J., Martin, J.L., 2005a. A natural experiment on the impact of overabundant deer on songbird populations. Biological Conservation 126, 1–13.
7. MacDougall, A.S., 2008. Herbivory, hunting, and long-term vegetation change in degraded savanna. Biological Conservation 141, 2174-2183.
8. Shackleton, D., 2000. Hoofed Mammals of British Columbia. Washington University Press, Vancouver.
9. Darimont, C.T., Price, M.H.H., Winchester, N.N., Gordon-walker, J., Paquet, P.C., 2004. Predators in natural fragments: foraging ecology of wolves in British Columbia's central and north coast archipelago. Journal of Biogeography 31, 1867–1877.
10. http://www.pzpinfo.org/home.html
11. Urban Ungulates Conflict Analysis FINAL July5–2010.pdf

In Iraq, Water Scarcity and Dam Building Threaten Migratory Birds

Environment News Service

The Environment News Service (ENS) is a daily international wire service of the environment. In the following viewpoint, ENS reports on the threats to migratory birds in Iraq's Euphrates and Tigris River basins. ENS says that this region is particularly important for migratory birds. The marshlands were deliberately drained during the 1990s by Iraqi dictator Saddam Hussein to punish those who lived there for political rebellion, but wetlands recovered somewhat after his regime was overthrown in 2003. Now, however, new dam and irrigation projects in the region are again spreading drought across the marshes. The result, says ENS, may be the destruction and extinction of migratory bird species.

As you read, consider the following questions:

1. What is World Migratory Bird Day, according to ENS?

2. According to ENS, what specific effects did Saddam Hussein's drainage and water diversion structures have on the Mesopotamian marshes?

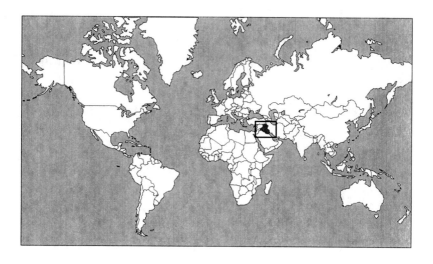

3. With what does Bert Lenten say that biodiversity provides humans?

To mark World Migratory Bird Day this Sunday [May 2010], the nongovernmental organization Nature Iraq is joining its BirdLife International partners around the world to celebrate bird migration and to highlight the difficulties facing some of the world's most threatened species.

Every Species Counts

The Mesopotamian marshes in the region of southern Iraq between the Euphrates and Tigris Rivers are especially important for wintering waterbirds, and Nature Iraq has worked to restore these marshes after they were 90 percent drained under [longtime Iraqi dictator] Saddam Hussein's regime. After several years of richer water flows, the marshes are again drying up because of drought and upstream dams.

"Iraq is, for good reasons, focused on security and development, but unless the country acts soon, many important species will simply not be here in 10 years' time," said Dr. Azzam Alwash, CEO [chief executive officer] of Nature Iraq.

World Migratory Bird Day is a global initiative to raise awareness of the need to conserve all migratory birds. This year's theme, "Save Migratory Birds in Crisis—Every Species Counts," is aimed at raising awareness of migratory birds on the very edge of extinction—the 31 species of birds classed as critically endangered by the International Union for Conservation of Nature, IUCN. Some of them depend on habitat in Iraq.

"In the Middle East, for example," warned Alwash, "the critically endangered sociable lapwing, *Vanellus gregarius*, could become extinct within a human generation due to persecution and habitat loss."

Once these birds bred in large numbers on open grassland in Russia and Kazakhstan, laying three to five eggs in nests on the ground. They migrated south through Kyrgyzstan, Tajikistan, Uzbekistan, Turkmenistan, Afghanistan, Armenia, Iran, Iraq, Saudi Arabia, Syria and Turkey, to key wintering sites in Israel, Syria, Eritrea, Sudan and northwestern India.

But in 2004, BirdLife International categorized the sociable lapwing as critically endangered, due to a rapid population decline for reasons not well understood.

The IUCN estimates a global population size of just 5,600 breeding pairs of sociable lapwings, or about 11,200 mature individuals, and projects the decline will continue.

Destroying Marshland

The Mesopotamian marshes grew hot and dry under the management of Saddam Hussein. After the first Gulf War [between Coalition forces, including the United States and Kuwait, and Iraq] ended in 1991, the regime built a series of drainage and water diversion structures that desiccated 90 percent of the world's then third-largest wetlands to punish a political rebellion by the Marsh Arabs [inhabitants of the Tigris-Euphrates marsh and region].

"During this time average temperatures in the area rose five degrees Celsius," said Dr. Alwash.

After the collapse of the regime in 2003, rehabilitation of the marshes began. As the hydro engineering structures were torn down, water flowed back into the internationally important wetlands, increasing the chances of survival for migratory birds in the region such as the Basra reed warbler, *Acrocephalus griseldis*, listed as endangered by the IUCN.

"The natural flow system is not going to return until and unless the dams outside Iraq are actively managed as part of a basin-wide coordinated management of the Tigris and Euphrates."

The Basra reed warbler breeds in the Mesopotamian marshes and winters in Sudan, Ethiopia, south Somalia, southeast Kenya, east Tanzania, southern Malawi and Mozambique.

But now the marshes are shrinking again as a result of drought and intensive dam construction and irrigation schemes upstream.

"Flooding has been disrupted by the dams built in Turkey, Syria and Iraq itself," observed Dr. Alwash last year. "The natural flow system is not going to return until and unless the dams outside Iraq are actively managed as part of a basin-wide coordinated management of the Tigris and Euphrates. In response, Nature Iraq is currently producing a drought management plan."

Dr. Michelle Stevens, assistant professor in the Environmental Studies Department of the California State University at Sacramento, wrote on her blog last year, "I have been a member of the Society of Wetland Scientists since the mid-1980s, and have worked in the wetlands field professionally since that time. The most compelling, heartbreaking and inspiring project I have ever worked on is the rehydration and now desiccation of the marshes of Iraq, and the adverse impacts on both the people of the marshes and the ecosystem."

The Marsh Arabs

Since Sumerian times, the traditional occupation of the Marsh Arabs has been fishing, and today over 80 per cent of those that have returned to re-flooded areas are engaged in the fishing industry. . . . Moreover, today's marshland returnees continue to face the problem of a total lack of the infrastructure required to support normal everyday life, including a lack of adequate safe drinking water, electricity, sewage treatment facilities, refuse collection and schools, clinics and other public facilities.

For many, life in the marshes was one of survival. The daily struggle with high temperatures, high humidity and seasonal flooding, in addition to trying to cope with a variety of insects, poisonous snakes, lack of drinking water and potential wild boar attacks turned the life of the marsh dweller into a scramble to stay alive. . . . Medical services, for example, were minimal and marsh dwellers often resorted to herbs to treat ailments, as is often found in traditional societies. Likewise, schools were difficult to build . . . and electricity was more a pipe dream than a reality.

Also, historically these wetlands were considered to be a main source of fresh water for human consumption, supplying communities living in and surrounding the marshes. This source gradually became contaminated until it was no longer suitable for human consumption. And since potable water was not available, the marsh dwellers were forced to drink the polluted marsh water. The destruction of the marshes has thus had severe human health consequences as a result of the loss of clean water and degradation of sanitation standards.

Sam A.A. Kubba and Abbas F. Jamali,
"History of the Iraqi Marshes,"
The Iraqi Marshlands and the Marsh Arabs;
The Ma'adan, Their Culture and the Environment.
Ed. Sam Kubba. Reading, United Kingdom: Ithaca Press, 2011.

Drought and Dam Building Affect Migration Routes

Dr. Stevens told ENS today that water scarcity in the Mesopotamian marshes is "a world-class disaster in the making."

"We believed that 20 percent of the marshes were left . . . but every time I talk to someone it's lower and lower."

"In southern Iraq there has been a precipitous emergency over lack of water," she said, partly because the Turkish government will continue construction of the Ilisu Dam on the Tigris River after receiving loans from three Turkish banks in January.

The Ilisu Dam is part of Turkey's Southeast Anatolia Project, an economic development program that plans for 22 dams and 19 hydroelectric projects to boost irrigated agriculture in Turkey's poor and arid southeastern corner, affecting the water available to downstream Iraq.

Iran has built a dam on the Karkheh River, which runs into Iraq. This water was diverted from the marshes just as they were declared to be a wetland of international importance under the Ramsar Convention.

"We believed that 20 percent of the marshes were left," said Stevens today, "but every time I talk to someone it's lower and lower. In the future we expect the situation to get much worse if there's no international agreement to allocate water to the marshes."

Iraq has established a national park in the central marshes, but Stevens says this area "may be some of the most vulnerable to upstream water drainage." The ducks that nest there in the summer would be particularly vulnerable, she said.

BirdLife partner organizations, such as Nature Iraq, network to help migratory birds to survive even under such adverse circumstances. "We operate in over 100 countries and territories worldwide, and work together to raise awareness about migratory birds and implement conservation projects," said Dr. Alwash.

"International collaboration is the only way to conserve migratory birds as they pass along their flyways," said Dr. Marco Lambertini, BirdLife's chief executive. "That's why the BirdLife partnership, with over 100 national organizations across the continents, can make a great difference in providing safer routes for migratory birds, as well as promoting the crucial intergovernmental coordinated efforts needed to address the growing threats along the flyways."

Bert Lenten, executive secretary of the African-Eurasian Waterbird Agreement [also known as the Agreement on the Conservation of African-Eurasian Migratory Waterbirds] and initiator of the World Migratory Bird Day campaign, said, "We know that migratory birds are part of the biological diversity of our world and are often used as indicators for the biological health of our ecosystems."

"We rely on this variety of life to provide us with the food, fuel, medicine and other essentials we simply cannot live without and it is in our power to protect these resources and to safeguard biodiversity," said Lenten.

To protect Iraq's biodiversity, Nature Iraq is conducting fieldwork to identify important bird areas and areas that are biologically diverse throughout the country.

And this weekend, the scientists, birding photographers, environmentalists, administrators, interpreters and translators, logistics experts, IT [information technology] and communication specialists of Nature Iraq will join thousands of other Iraqis at peaceful events such as bird festivals, education programs and trips to watch birds migrate.

In Japan, Invasive Fish Species Threaten Biodiversity

Mizuho Aoki

Mizuho Aoki is a staff writer for the Japan Times. *In the following viewpoint, she reports that North American fish species such as black bass and bluegill have proliferated in Japanese ponds and waterways, threatening native species with extinction. Aoki says that nonnative fish often get into ponds and rivers when people tire of keeping them as pets and release them into the wild. Conservation groups have worked to catch bluegill and black bass and are also trying to educate the Japanese people about the dangers of releasing nonnative species. However, progress is slow, and Aoki concludes that at best it will take decades for native species to make a comeback in Japan.*

As you read, consider the following questions:

1. How many bluegill and black bass were caught by the Inokashira Nature Watchers group between 2007 and April 2012, according to Aoki?
2. How does Aoki say that bluegill were introduced into Japan?
3. What is the Osakana Post, and how does it help prevent the distribution of nonnative species of fish into the Tama River?

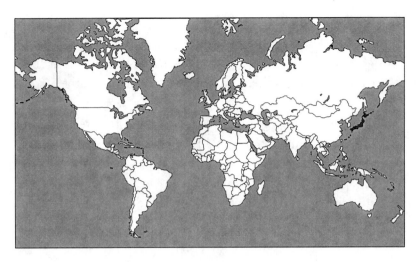

Looking at black bass and bluegill caught fresh at Inokashira Park, Toshiaki Tanaka sighed with satisfaction at catching some of the nonnative species plaguing its picturesque pond. But at the same time, he said he was frustrated knowing that alien species remain firmly entrenched there despite the five years he and his friends have spent trying to fish them out.

Bluegill and Black Bass Expand in Numbers

"If nothing is done, this pond will be packed only with black bass and bluegill. . . . The balance of creatures in the park will be destroyed," he said.

Tanaka, 59, heads the Inokashira Nature Watchers group, a nonprofit organization promoting biodiversity in the park, an oasis of cherry trees and fresh air straddling the cities of Mitaka and Musashino in Tokyo's western suburbs.

Starting in 2007, with approval from the Tokyo Metropolitan Government, the group began capturing bluegill and black bass—freshwater species indigenous to North America—in the pond to protect its native species and ecosystem.

As of April 21, [2012,] the group's 23 members had caught a total of 289,101 bluegill and 24,309 bass. Their efforts, though low-key, have been effective in preventing the foreign fish from expanding their numbers—and saving native breeds from extinction.

Nevertheless, the group hasn't been able to effect a major drop in the invaders' population or reverse the decline in indigenous species.

"There are limits to what we can do," Tanaka said. "The reproductive power of black bass and bluegills is high."

Foreign Invaders

Inokashira pond is just one of many rivers, lakes and other inland bodies of water suffering from growing numbers of foreign fish threatening native species that have existed for centuries.

Black bass initially entered Japan in 1925 via Lake Ashinoko in Kanagawa Prefecture, followed by the first bluegill in 1960, according to Environment Ministry data. The bass were apparently released by people who enjoy bass fishing, while the bluegill were released as bait, experts say.

The bluegill were reportedly brought from the U.S. to Japan as a gift in 1960 by Emperor Akihito when he was the Crown Prince, and given to a fisheries agency research institute for consideration as a food fish.

With their high reproductive power, the populations of the two fish exploded nationwide in the 1990s. By 2001, black bass had been spotted in all 47 prefectures and had established habitats everywhere except in Hokkaido, according to the ministry. Bluegill have also been confirmed in most prefectures.

To prevent further invasion, the Environment Ministry instituted the Invasive Alien Species Act in 2004 to ban the breeding, holding, transport and import of foreign species, including bass and bluegill. At present, the law covers 13 species.

Many other nonnative species spotted in Japan are spreading as unwanted pets released by disenchanted pet lovers. These include the guppy, a tiny tropical fish, and even vicious snapping turtles, both of which have been spotted in Inokashira Park.

Today, Inokashira pond is almost dominated by bluegill and bass. The native species, including the stone "moroko" (a type of carp) and the "toyoshinobori" rhinogobius, are in decline.

The metropolitan government also plans to drain the pond to clean the muddy water and to eliminate foreign species.

In the meantime, Tanaka said that the park's "kaitsuburi" (dabchicks), which depend on the stone moroko as food, are nearly gone.

"A few years ago, there were three breeding pairs of dabchick (in the park). But now only one pair remains," he said of the ducks.

Last fall, the Tokyo Metropolitan Government blocked off a corner of the pond to build a protected space where native fish species can live and hopefully breed. Tanaka said he is eager to see indigenous species flourish again but hasn't been able to confirm an uptick in the population yet.

The metropolitan government also plans to drain the pond to clean the muddy water and to eliminate foreign species. A similar method was used a few times in the moat around the Imperial Palace and had been considered effective in eliminating the two interlopers.

However, Norio Iwami, a professor of environmental microbiology at Meisei University, said it's anyone's guess how long that measure will work.

"By draining the water, we can clearly see what kind of creatures are living in the pond and we can retrieve them. So it would be effective," Iwami said. "But if an Adam and Eve remain, they breed again. If they can't retrieve all the eggs, then I don't know what will happen. We'll have to wait for a year or two to know the result."

The Fish Post

Meanwhile, another conservation group has been taking different measures to protect indigenous species in the Tama River, which some have dubbed the "Tamazon" because of the many abandoned tropical fish spotted in it.

Mitsuaki Yamasaki, one of the leaders of Osakana Post, a nonprofit environmental organization based in Kawasaki, has been calling on people to dump unwanted fish in a tank it installed in the city instead of releasing them into the Tama.

"The Tama River used to be home to some 50 native species. But now some 250 species, including foreign ones, have been confirmed."

Since the "osakana post" (fish post) was set up in Kawasaki in 2005, about 10,000 fish, including gar and axolotl, have been dumped into the tank each year, with many donated to schools . . . .

Yamasaki looks after about 1,000 of the fish at his home in Kawasaki. Although it costs him about ¥150,000 in electricity each month, he said his concerns for the river and his love of the fish keep him going.

"The Tama River used to be home to some 50 native species. But now some 250 species, including foreign ones, have been confirmed," he said.

"What people don't realize is that they live for a long time. For example, catfish live for 40 or 50 years and carp live for about 50 to 80 years," he said. "People should think more seriously about whether they can look after such fish for such a long time before purchasing them."

Educating people and discouraging them from dumping fish into the wild are the only ways the group can protect indigenous species, he said.

Thanks to the fish post and educational efforts, Yamasaki said almost no foreign species can be spotted around Kawasaki. But in other areas, things are about the same.

"Unlike the pond, we cannot drain water from a river. So the important thing is to stop people from dumping fish. Also, in the case of the highly reproductive black bass and bluegill, we have to capture them to some extent," he said.

By doing that, native species may someday outnumber nonnative ones in the Tama—in 50 or 100 years, Yamasaki said.

In Taiwan, Overfishing Threatens Marine Biodiversity and Is Not Sustainable

Kwang-Tsao Shao

Kwang-Tsao Shao is a research fellow with the Biodiversity Research Center, Academia Sinica in Taipei, Taiwan. In the following viewpoint, he argues that marine fish are vital as a source of food for humans. However, environmental protection of aquatic resources has lagged well behind protection of land resources. As a result, he says, marine fisheries are in danger of collapsing, with devastating effects on human populations. He points in particular to Taiwan, a center of marine biodiversity, where fish populations and fish biodiversity have been dropping dangerously. He suggests that Taiwan needs to reduce overfishing; increase protected areas; and improve education, research, and government policies to preserve its fisheries.

As you read, consider the following questions:

1. What was the fishery production of Taiwan in 1995, and why does Shao say it has decreased since then?

2. What two factors does Shao say help to explain Taiwan's marine biodiversity?

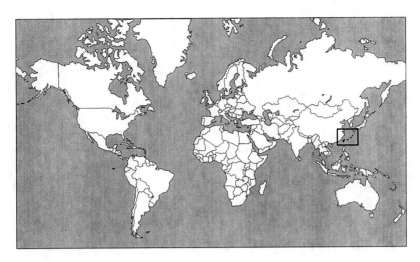

3. According to Shao, what should help to increase Taiwanese public awareness of marine ecology?

Marine fish is one of the most important sources of animal protein for human use, especially in developing countries with coastlines. Marine fishery is also an important industry in many countries. Fifty years ago, many people believed that the ocean was so vast and so resilient that there was no way the marine environment could be changed, nor could marine fishery resources be depleted. Half a century later, we all agree that the depletion of fishery resources is happening mainly due to anthropogenic [that is, human] factors such as overfishing, habitat destruction, pollution, invasive species introduction, and climate change. Since overfishing can cause chain reactions that decrease marine biodiversity drastically, there will be no seafood left after 40 years if we take no action. The most effective ways to reverse this downward trend and restore fishery resources are to promote fishery conservation, establish marine-protected areas, adopt ecosystem-based management, and implement a "precautionary principle." Additionally, enhancing public awareness of marine conservation, which includes eco-labeling, fishery ban or enclosure, slow fishing, and MPA (marine protected areas) enforcement, is important and effective. In this [viewpoint], we use Taiwan as an example to discuss the problems facing marine biodiversity and sustainable fisheries.

Fisheries and Taiwan

The ocean covers 70 percent of the earth's surface area, but it can provide more than 98 percent of the volume of the biosphere. Marine fishery resources are one of the most important animal protein sources for human health, reaching 19 percent of our total protein intake. According to FAO [Food and Agriculture Organization of the United Nations] statistics, world fishery production has declined since the 1980s and can maintain only about 100 million tons each year. Of this, 76 percent is used directly for human consumption. The remaining 24 percent is used for fish meal, much of it for aquaculture. There are about 200 million people whose livelihood and income depend on fisheries.

In the past, most people believed that marine fisheries were inexhaustible. However, they never thought it might be true only with traditional fishing methods and artisanal fisheries of their time period. After the industrial revolution, and the rapid development of science and technology, modernistic fish-detecting devices and fishing techniques have left fish with no way to hide. The great sea fisheries have undergone serious overexploitation because of increased seafood demand driven by rapid growth of the human population. It is widely believed that the collapse of global fishery resources has been mainly due to inappropriate fishery management and the falling behind of marine conservation in comparison to terrestrial conservation. For example, people will not feel guilty eating tuna, shark, or grouper. But they will if they eat tiger, lion, or hawk. Marine fishery is the only industry left where people are still hunting from the wild. In contrast, agriculture, forestry, and animal husbandry are all industries where people harvest plants they grow or animals they keep in captivity.

In Taiwan, overall fishery production was only 0.2 million tons per year in 1950, but increased to 1.2 million tons by 1990, and 1.3 million tons in 1995 with a value of nearly NT$100 billion. This led Taiwan to be ranked among the top 20 fishery producers in the world. The catch has decreased continuously since then simply because of the paucity of fishes. Sport fishing, collecting fish and shellfish for the aquarium trade, and illegal fishing using explosives, poisons, electricity, and other destructive methods are gradually destroying the marine ecosystem.

More than one-tenth of the world's marine species are found in Taiwan.

In 1990, 130,000 of Taiwan's households, or approximately 300,000 people, were involved in fisheries. Fishing has contributed greatly to social stability on the island, and fish is an important source of food. However, production began to decline in 1990, especially in coastal and offshore fisheries. These two fisheries combined only account for less than 17 percent of total fishery production (far sea fisheries 58 percent, aquaculture 25 percent) in 2007. Destruction of the marine environment and the degradation of the marine ecosystem are the obvious causes of the decline, especially in the coastal area. The sustainability of marine resources depends on the extent that we effectively protect our marine environment and manage our fisheries.

Taiwan is a relatively small island, but it is rich in marine biodiversity. More than one-tenth of the world's marine species are found in Taiwan. The total number of marine fish species exceeds 3,000. Comparing Taiwan's land area to the world's total, the marine species biodiversity is approximately 400 times the average number of species in other countries.

The following two factors explain Taiwan's rich marine biodiversity:

1. Geographically, Taiwan is located at the northern border of the East Indies—the world's marine biodiversity center, which includes Indonesia, Borneo, and the Philippines. Taiwan is also located at the apex of the Coral Triangle. Many eggs, larvae, juveniles, and even adults are easily transported to Taiwan waters via the Kuroshio and South China Sea ocean currents.

2. Ecologically, Taiwan has various kinds of marine habitats. The island's west coast mangrove forests, estuaries, and sandy barrier lagoons are characterized by sandy bottoms; the northern and southern tips of Taiwan and the islets of Penghu, Hsiao Liuchiu, Green Island, and Orchid Island are characterized by coral reefs; and the east coast is dominated by rocky shores and open ocean (deep sea). Water depth ranges from an average of 50 m [meters] in the Taiwan Strait between Taiwan and Mainland China, to a couple thousand meters off Taiwan's east coast. Three main ocean currents—Kuroshio, China Coast Current, and the South China Sea current—flow and intersect in the waters around Taiwan, which results in a water temperature difference of at least 6–7 degrees between northern and southern Taiwan. The dominant marine species thus vary significantly between northern and southern Taiwan.

Causes of Marine Ecosystem Destruction

Increase in the number of species has not led to a corresponding increase in fishery resources. In fact, the abundance of most species has declined drastically. Many species that were common 20 years ago have now become occasional or rare. Decreasing biodiversity leads to the degradation of marine ecosystems and a decline in fishery productions. The main causes include (1) overfishing and bycatches, (2) habitat destruction, (3) pollution, (4) introduced species, and (5) natural perturbation. The first four causes are related to fisheries and are considered anthropogenic perturbations.

Overfishing and bycatches. Fishing obviously has direct effects on fish stocks. It can alter the abundance, age and size structures, sex ratio, and the genetic structure of the target fish population. The species composition of marine communities is also affected. Noncommercial species (those species that are smaller, less abundant, and less valuable) are discarded. The waste associated with this bycatch problem can reach 9/10 of all harvests, as in prawn (shrimp) trawling. This is the main cause of commercial extinction. Although incidental catches of [International Union for Conservation of Nature] IUCN-protected species of marine mammals, sea turtles, and sea birds have received much attention, many long-lived marine species with low fecundity, large pelagic species such as tuna, swordfish, dolphinfish, ocean sunfish, and sharks, and some demersal species such as groupers are still not adequately protected.

Habitat destruction. Species cannot survive and resources cannot be sustained without the habitats necessary for reproduction, feeding, and sheltering during each stage of their life cycles. Unfortunately, Taiwan's natural coastal wetlands are gradually being destroyed by urbanization and the construction of shore-based or near-shore facilities, such as fishing harbors, industrial or recreational parks, and wave breaks. The natural coastline of Isla Formosa is going to become "Isla Artificial," surrounded by a man-made concrete coastline if the progress isn't halted. Eventually, the all-important nursery grounds for many economic and noneconomic species of marine organisms will be destroyed.

Fishing can also affect habitats, most notably by destroying and disturbing benthic [that is, sea bottom] topography and associated communities. Bottom trawlers in Taiwan—nearly 2000 boats in 2001—have damaged the benthic ecosystem seriously. This damage extends to coral reefs. Large-scale mariculture activities (farming of fish, shrimp, and other marine organisms)—especially if they are poorly managed—can also negatively impact marine ecosystems through damage to coastal wetlands and near-shore ecosystems.

Pollution. Marine pollution is caused by organic and inorganic pollutants, including heavy metals, oil, and other toxic substances. Sewage stemming from industry, agriculture, and urbanization, and soil runoffs due to deforestation and unplanned agriculture can also damage marine ecosystems by increasing suspension particles and turbidity in seawater, especially in coral reef areas. Fishery activities can also be a source of pollution. In mariculture areas, the marine ecosystem can be changed through eutrophication [an ecosystem response to the addition of artificial substances] and the contamination of the water by food, antibiotics, and waste, and through the introduction of diseases and exotic genotypes.

Introduced species. Taiwanese researchers have yet to conduct a survey of alien marine species introduced from ballast waters, but one introduced species, red drum (*Sciaenops ocellatus*), for cage-net harvesting, has been discovered off western Taiwan.

Natural perturbation. The source of natural perturbation can be summed up as follows: (1) Strong typhoons can destroy fragile coral species in shallow waters, and consequently impact fish species living in close association with the coral. (2) Cold water masses, which occasionally enter the coastal region in the winter season, can kill marine fishes. This has occurred frequently in Penghu (Pescadores Islands), and occasionally in Kenting, in southern Taiwan. One recent massive kill of fishes by cold water intrusion happened in 2008.

Conservation Strategies

Natural perturbation is impossible to prevent, but anthropogenic causes are avoidable through enhanced public educa-

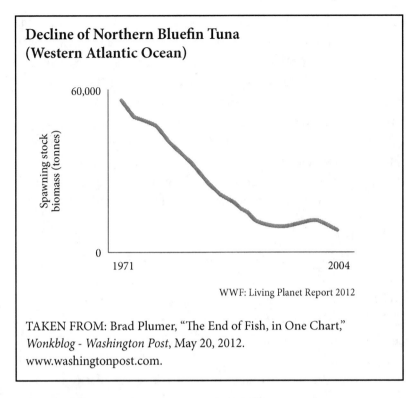

Decline of Northern Bluefin Tuna (Western Atlantic Ocean)

Spawning stock biomass (tonnes)

60,000

0

1971   2004

WWF: Living Planet Report 2012

TAKEN FROM: Brad Plumer, "The End of Fish, in One Chart," *Wonkblog - Washington Post*, May 20, 2012. www.washingtonpost.com.

tion, monitoring, and assessment, and through the establishment of effective conservation policies.

Reducing overfishing. Managing single-species fisheries with an explicitly conservative approach could be a first step toward achieving sustainable marine fisheries. A moderate level of exploitation might be a better goal for fisheries than full exploitation. Recreational fishing, diving, and fish watching are less destructive than commercial fishing and can potentially generate more revenue if managed effectively.

Taiwanese people love to eat seafood, but they are loving it to death.

Marine protected areas (MPAs). The most effective way to protect and rebuild the ecosystem and increase marine resources is to establish more MPAs. It has been shown that the establishment of such protected areas increases the number of fish and other species in nearby waters. The design and implementation of MPAs should convince fishermen that the resulting system will protect their long-term interests. Fishing industry participation in planning also improves operational integrity. Recent calls for protecting 20 percent of potential fishing areas before year 2020 provide a worthwhile reference point for future consideration and emphasize the importance of greatly expanding the areas currently protected.

Although more than 70 marine sanctuaries have been established in Taiwan, they have not been managed or controlled appropriately. These MPAs include 7 wildlife sanctuaries, 3 natural reserves, 26 resource conservation areas, and 12 coastal protected zones. Conservation efforts in these areas are only focused on protecting mangroves, seabirds, and sea turtles, as well as economic species such as seaweeds, lobsters, abalones, and bivalves. Despite the fact that they are not real MPAs and do not protect the entire habitat, artificial reefs built as part of conservation efforts have created more shelters for juvenile fishes and have reduced illegal bottom trawler fishing within 3 nautical miles of them.

Enhancing public education. Taiwanese people love to eat seafood, but they are loving it to death. The inclusion of many rare and endangered marine organisms on menus is putting them in jeopardy. The government must enhance public awareness through the media to educate people not to catch, raise, and eat rare or protected species. Fortunately, the number of NGOs [nongovernmental organizations] that actively promote marine conservation in Taiwan is increasing. Also, several large marine aquariums and museums have opened recently, with several more under construction, which allow people to get acquainted with marine organisms. Interpretive exhibits in these museums should go a long way toward increasing public awareness of conservation issues. Whale watching, snorkeling, and establishment of green sea turtle sanctuaries also increase awareness.

Enhance research. Better understanding of the structure and functioning of marine ecosystems is needed, including the role of the habitat and factors affecting stability and resilience. This includes attempting to understand mechanisms at lower levels of the organization (i.e., populations and communities), long-term research and monitoring programs, and the development of trophic ecosystem models. More research is needed on basic taxonomy, ecology, and distribution. These basic data should be integrated using a geographical information system (GIS) and be made available to the public via the Internet. The biological effects of fishing, such as the alteration of gene pools and population structures as a consequence of fishing, need to be studied as well. More research is needed on the conditions under which MPAs are most effective, and MPAs themselves should be used as research tools. More information is needed on the effects and effectiveness of various management regimes, including rights-based management approaches.

Legislation and policies. There are four laws governing marine conservation in Taiwan: National Park Law (1972); Cultural Heritage Preservation Law (1982); Wildlife Conservation Law (1989); and Environmental Impact [Assessment] Act (1994). Each of these laws provides some legal basis for the protection of the marine ecosystem, but regulations stemming from these laws are rarely enforced. Most previously established sanctuaries and natural reserves have focused on a few endangered or economically important species, not on the habitat as a whole; thus, their benefits can easily be called into question.

Over the past few years, the government and private organizations have recognized the importance of marine conservation and have started to change policies to provide increased environmental protection. However, legislative Yuan [the Taiwan legislative body] has not been able to approve the law of coast management in the past 10 years. People are still eating coral fishes and enjoying tuna and shark fins, ignoring the fact that their resources are declining. Adding more marine species to the aquatic trade red list should prove useful as well.

The following current marine conservation issues should be stressed here:

1. Marine environmental awareness is much lower than terrestrial awareness—in Taiwan, this problem seems to be even more serious than in foreign countries.

2. Economy vs. environment dilemma—conflict between the construction of the industrial complex and saving endangered species such as the black-faced spoonbill and the Chinese white dolphin.

3. The difficulty of establishing new MPAs and marine reserves, and the lack of enforcement.

In Antarctica, Fishing Fleets Threaten Albatross Species

Becky Allen

Becky Allen writes regularly for the website of the British Antarctic Survey. In the following viewpoint, she reports that albatross species are declining to dangerous levels. Albatross mature slowly and lay eggs relatively infrequently; therefore, their populations can be particularly vulnerable. Allen says that the birds have been harmed by fishing fleets, which release long lines baited with hooks that can catch and drown albatross. Having identified the danger to the albatross, scientists have had some luck in convincing fleets to change their practices so that albatross are not accidentally caught. However, Allen concludes, albatross populations have not yet rebounded, requiring more work to be done in this area of conservation.

As you read, consider the following questions:

1. Why does Dr. Richard Phillips say that everything that albatrosses do is slow?

2. According to Phillips, what makes the South Georgia albatross population the best studied worldwide?

3. What mitigation measures does Phillips say can be put in place to prevent killing of albatrosses by fishing fleets?

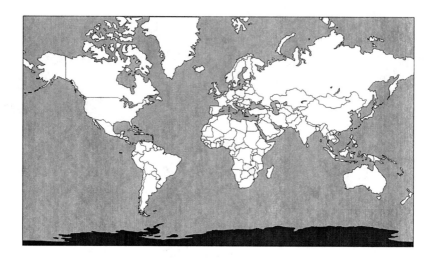

Albatrosses are the stuff of legend. Immortalised in Samuel Taylor Coleridge's [1798 poem] *The Rime of the Ancient Mariner,* and once thought to contain the souls of sailors lost at sea, it's easy to see why the albatross has become such an iconic species.

According to Dr Richard Phillips of British Antarctic Survey (BAS), the sight of an albatross at sea, thousands of miles from land, is a very special experience: "Albatrosses will often follow ships, sometimes for days on end. Seeing these beautiful great, white birds flying off the back of the ship you're on really captures people's imaginations."

Albatrosses are among the largest flying birds on earth. With their massive wingspan, they spend most of their lives at sea.

Patrolling some of the remotest oceans on the planet, albatrosses can travel up to 1,000 miles a day in search of food and can circumnavigate the Southern Ocean 30 times or more during their 60-year life span.

Heading for Extinction

But it is this extraordinary lifestyle—coupled with humans' insatiable appetite for tuna and other fish—that is putting most species of albatross at risk of extinction.

Because they are almost as long-lived as humans, albatrosses take many years to reach sexual maturity. An albatross will be around 10 years old before it finds a mate and breeds. Although most breed annually, nine species—including the wandering albatross—lay only one egg every two years, and it takes the best part of a year for a young albatross to leave the nest.

"Everything they do is slow," says Phillips, who has spent the last seven years studying the albatrosses breeding at South Georgia. "It takes a long time for them to raise a chick, the chick takes a long time to learn how to forage, and it won't breed successfully until it's 10 years old or more. If you do the math, you have to have enough birds surviving that early period and producing enough chicks to sustain the population. And because chick production is so slow, even a small increase in the death rate among adults will cause the population to decline."

Sadly, the picture that this science paints is one of inexorably declining albatross numbers.

Bird Island

Scientists at BAS have been monitoring albatross populations at its research station at Bird Island, South Georgia, since the early 1960s. Lying off the northwest tip of South Georgia, Bird Island is a rocky, windswept island just five kilometres long. Its only human inhabitants are the handful of BAS scientists who work there studying the thousands of seals, albatrosses and other birds that use the island to breed on.

BAS monitors populations of three albatross species—the wandering albatross, the black-browed albatross and the grey-headed albatross—on Bird Island. Together with South Georgia, it is home to some of the largest colonies of these birds in the world. "The biggest global populations of grey-headed and

The Albatross May Aid Worldwide Conservation Efforts

Add the problems of overfishing and illegal fishing to the capacity of long-line and trawl fishing for killing large numbers of seabirds, and the threat to seabirds seems overwhelming. However, there is a hopeful note in the linkage of the fate of the albatross with the fate of commercially desirable fish as well as the marine environment. This fact is what makes saving the albatross more than single-species conservation. Consider the commitments, resources, persuasion, and opportunity costs of efforts to protect the spotted owl in the northwest forests of the United States, or the golden-cheeked warbler and black-capped vireo in the Southwest. And then expand your mental reach to consider the seemingly insurmountable challenges of attempting to protect a truly international and global wanderer such as the albatross. The birds' connection with marine environments . . . has provided a solid rationale for an international commitment of time and resources to saving albatrosses. But there are solid rationales for all kinds of beneficial actions on the part of governments. The amazing thing is that once the problem was identified as the connection between albatrosses and commercial fishing, in a relatively short period of time in terms of environmental progress, an international environmental regime took shape to save the albatross.

Robin W. Doughty and Virginia Carmichael,
The Albatross and the Fish: Linked Lives in the Open Seas.
Austin: University of Texas Press, 2011.

light-mantled albatrosses are on South Georgia, which also has the second largest populations of wandering albatrosses and black-browed albatrosses, so South Georgia is a very important breeding site," Phillips explains.

"South Georgia albatross populations are among the best studied worldwide. For wandering albatross, BAS has a high-intensity study area of about 120 pairs. We have ringed all the adults here and we monitor laying dates, egg size, hatching success, chick growth and fledging success. And from resighting adults in successive years we get an indication of how often they breed and of adult survival," Phillips says.

Sadly, the picture that this science paints is one of inexorably declining albatross numbers. According to Phillips: "The populations that are declining most rapidly are in the South Atlantic, breeding on the UK Overseas Territories. On South Georgia, the three species that BAS monitors are declining at between 2% and 5% a year."

Crucially in conservation terms, it is the satellite transmitters and tiny geolocators they attach to the birds that have given BAS scientists an unparalleled insight into why albatross populations are declining so dramatically.

"Around South Georgia during the late 1990s there were 6,000 seabirds being killed each year. But the introduction of the various mitigation measures ... has been so successful that last year no birds were killed."

Fatal Fisheries

Data from these devices show that the birds are feeding for the fish and squid on which they depend in the same areas in which fishing fleets operate. Both trawling and long-lining—where fishing vessels release lines containing thousands of baited hooks—are killing thousands of albatrosses each year. Attracted to the bait on the hooks, many albatrosses will swallow fishing hooks and drown behind long-line fishing vessels, while others will collide with trawler cables, breaking their wings and falling into the sea.

But by understanding why, where and when the birds are being killed in such large numbers, scientists have been able to suggest ways in which fisheries can operate successfully at the same time as mitigating the impact on the albatrosses.

According to Phillips: "Once people realised long-lining was a threat, there was a lot of effort to develop different ways for mitigating that threat. You can have a streamer line flapping behind the vessel to discourage birds from trying to feed on the baited hooks. You can weight hooks so that they sink quickly below the surface and become inaccessible to birds. You can set the baits underwater, keep offal and waste bait on board so that you don't encourage birds to come to the boat in the first place, and set the lines during the night, when albatrosses don't usually feed. And around South Georgia, there's also a closed season, so they don't fish during the summer when the smaller species are vulnerable."

The success of these measures in eliminating so-called "bycatch" of albatrosses around South Georgia gives Phillips grounds for hope: "Around South Georgia during the late 1990s there were 6,000 seabirds being killed each year. But the introduction of the various mitigation measures, which were made mandatory by the South Georgia government, has been so successful that last year no birds were killed. It's an example of a very profitable fishery which has successfully introduced mitigation measures, and which was recently accorded Marine Stewardship Council certification in recognition of its high level of environmental sustainability and management."

The challenge now is to ensure that other fisheries follow suit. "What's unfortunate is that because these birds migrate vast distances, they still encounter fishing fleets in other areas of ocean that aren't using mitigation measures. What we have to do now is to persuade the Regional Fisheries Management Organisation—the big tuna commissions—to take a stronger approach to enforcing mitigation measures. Things are looking up, but as yet we haven't seen an upturn in the populations in the South Atlantic, so there's still a lot of work to be done," Phillips says.

Periodical and Internet Sources Bibliography

The following articles have been selected to supplement the diverse views presented in this chapter.

Jane Arraf	"A New Effort to Preserve Iraq's Rich Biodiversity, from Mountains to Marshes," *Christian Science Monitor*, October 28, 2010.
Sabri Ben-Achour	"Growing Deer Population Hurts Survival of Forests," NPR, June 15, 2011. http://www.npr.org/2011/06/15/137192604/what-does-more-deer-mean-for-forests.
Victoria Gill	"Chernobyl Zone Shows Decline in Biodiversity," BBC News, July 30, 2010. http://www.bbc.co.uk/news/science-environment-10819027.
Andrew C. Revkin	"An Albatross's Flight from Extinction's Edge," *Dot Earth* (blog), *New York Times*, April 20, 2012. http://dotearth.blogs.nytimes.com/2012/04/20/an-albatrosss-flight-from-extinctions-edge.
Thomas P. Rooney	"What Do We Do with Too Many White-Tailed Deer?," Actionbioscience.org, May 2010. http://www.actionbioscience.org/biodiversity/rooney.html.
Mort Rosenblum and Mar Cabra	"In Mackerel's Plunder, Hints of Epic Fish Collapse," *New York Times*, January 25, 2012.
Jessica Ruvinsky	"Chernobyl: A Biodiversity Hot Spot?," *Discover*, January 21, 2006.
ScienceDaily	"Fishery Collapse Near Venezuela Linked to Climate Change," October 18, 2012. http://www.sciencedaily.com/releases/2012/10/121018094853.htm.

 GLOBALVIEWPOINTS

CHAPTER

Biodiversity and Agriculture

Biodiversity Can Help Agriculture Adapt to Climate Change

Janet Cotter and Reyes Tirado

Janet Cotter and Reyes Tirado are both honorary research fellows at Greenpeace Research Laboratories at the University of Exeter. In the following viewpoint, they argue that genetic biodiversity—that is, multiple strains of a single crop—can help crops withstand varied conditions and natural disasters. Thus, biodiversity is vital for agriculture to withstand the great changes that will result from global climate change. The authors say that, in contrast, there is little scientific evidence that genetically engineered, or GE, crops will respond well to global warming.

As you read, consider the following questions:

1. What do the authors say are among the more drastic changes that would affect food production as the climate warms?

2. According to the authors, what did agronomists find when comparing corn yields between fields planted as monocultures and fields planted with a greater range of genetic diversity?

3. Why can plants produced with marker assisted selection alone not be counted on to provide food security, according to the authors?

Some of the most profound and direct impacts of climate change over the next few decades will be on agriculture and food systems. All quantitative assessments show that climate change will adversely affect food security.

Impact of Climate Change on Agriculture and Food Security

Increasing temperatures, declining and more unpredictable rainfall, more frequent extreme weather and higher severity of pest and disease are among the more drastic changes that would impact food production. However, global trends mask tremendous regional differences, with the poorest being most at risk both by global climate variations and global commodity price fluctuations. Some of the most important effects of global climate change will be felt among smallholder farmers, predominantly in developing countries.

The latest Intergovernmental Panel on Climate Change (IPCC) report predicts the probability of more heat waves, heavy rainfall, droughts and other extreme weather throughout the 21st century.

Warming in the Indian Ocean and an increasingly "El Niño-like" climate [that is, a climate pattern that occurs across the South Pacific that creates increased rainfall in the Southern Hemisphere] could reduce main-season precipitation across most of Africa, East and South Asia, and Central and South America.

It has been shown that by 2080, the 40 poorest countries, located predominantly in tropical Africa and Latin America, could lose 10 to 20 percent of their basic grain growing capacity due to drought. The biggest problem for food security will be the predicted increase in extreme weather, which will damage crops at particular developmental stages and make the timing of farming more difficult, reducing farmers' incentives to cultivate.

There is abundant scientific evidence that crop biodiversity has an important role to play in the adaptation to our changing environment.

Biodiversity—A Natural Insurance Policy Against Climate Change

Diversity farming is the single most important modern technology to achieve food security in a changing climate. Scientists have shown that diversity provides a natural insurance policy against major ecosystem changes, be it in the wild or in agriculture. It is now predicted that genetic diversity will be most crucial in highly variable environments and those under rapid human-induced climate change.

The larger the number of different species or varieties present in one field or in an ecosystem, the greater the probability that at least some of them can cope with changing conditions. Species diversity also reduces the probability of pests and diseases by diluting the availability of their hosts. It is an age-old insurance policy of farming communities to hedge their risks and plant diverse crops or varieties. The strategy is not to maximise yield in an optimum year, but to maximise yield over years, good and bad, by decreasing the chance of crop failure in a bad year.

This diversification strategy is backed by a wealth of recent scientific data:

- In a unique cooperation project among Chinese scientists and farmers in Yunnan during 1998 and 1999, researchers calculated the effect of diversity on the severity of rice blast, the major disease of rice. They showed that disease-susceptible rice varieties planted with resistant varieties had an 89 percent greater yield than when they were grown in a monoculture. Mixed varieties of rice produced more grain per hectare than their corresponding monocultures in all cases; close to 20 percent more land is needed in a monoculture to produce the same amount of hybrid and glutinous rice as was produced in a mixture. The experiment was so successful that fungicidal sprays were no longer applied by the end of the two-year programme. The practice expanded to more than 40,000 hectares in 2000, and now includes some varieties that were formerly locally extinct. This is especially remarkable as the yield gains were on top of already high average yields in the region, at nearly 10 tonnes per hectare, among the highest in the world. This shows that greater rice diversity means lower rates of plant disease and greater yields while conserving genetic diversity, all at minimal cost for farmers and the environment.

- Off the German coast, a genetically diverse area of sea grass was not only able to survive a heat wave, but experienced 26–34 percent more growth than sea grass monocultures, showing how genetic diversity increases the ability for plants to recover after a perturbation, while genetic monocultures have a limited short-term ability to respond to extreme climatic events.

- In Italy, a high level of genetic diversity within wheat fields on nonirrigated farms reduces risk of crop failure during dry conditions. A scenario where rainfall declines by 20 percent, the wheat yield would fall sharply, but when diversity is increased by 2 percent, this decline cannot only be reversed but above average yields achieved.

- Agronomists in the United States compared corn yields between fields planted as monocultures and those with various levels of intercropping in Michigan over three years. They found the yields in fields with the highest diversity (three crops, plus three cover crops) were over 100 percent higher than in continuous monocultures. Crop diversity improved soil fertility, reducing the need to use chemical inputs while maintaining high yields.

There is abundant scientific evidence that crop biodiversity has an important role to play in the adaptation to our changing environment. While oversimplified farming systems, such as monocultures of genetically identical plants, would not be able to cope with a changing climate, increasing the biodiversity of an agro-ecosystem can help maintain its long-term productivity and contribute significantly to food security. Genetic diversity within a field provides a buffer against losses caused by environmental change, pests and diseases. Genetic diversity provides the resilience needed for reliable and stable, long-term food production.

Analysis of past environment changes that resulted in dramatic famines (e.g., Ireland's potato famine [in the nineteenth century] and Ethiopia 1965–1997) shows specialised monocultures are highly vulnerable.

In addition to enhancing food security and climate resilience, diversity in the field also delivers important ecosystem services. Variety mixtures that are tolerant to drought and flood not only increase productivity, but also prevent soil erosion and desertification, increase soil organic matter and help stabilise slopes. Benefits for farmers include reducing the need for costly pesticides, receiving price premiums for valued traditional varieties and improving their dietary diversity and health.

GE Crops Contribute to Climate Change

Industrial globalized agriculture is heavily implicated in climate change. It contributes to the three major greenhouse gases: carbon dioxide (CO_2) from the use of fossil fuels, nitrogen oxide (N_2O) from the use of chemical fertilizers and methane (CH_4) from factory farming. . . . The global atmospheric concentration of N_2O, largely due to use of chemical fertilizers in agriculture, increased from about 270 parts per billion to 319 parts per billion in 2005. Industrial agriculture is also more vulnerable to climate change, which is intensifying droughts and floods.

Monocultures lead to more frequent crop failure when rainfall does not come in time, or is too much or too little. Chemically fertilized soils have no capacity to withstand a drought. And cyclones and hurricanes make a food system dependent on long-distance transport highly vulnerable to disruption. Genetic engineering is embedded in an industrial model of agriculture based on fossil fuels. It is falsely being offered as a magic bullet for dealing with climate change.

Vandana Shiva,
"Climate Change and Agriculture,"
The Global Warming Reader:
A Century of Writing About Climate Change.
Ed. Bill McKibben. New York: Penguin, 2012.

Modern Breeding Techniques for Diverse Genetics Traits

In addition to increasing the diversity of crops and varieties in a single field, increasing the diversity of traits within one variety might help climate change adaptation. If each of the single varieties in one field has a higher tolerance to droughts, salinity, floods, storms and pests, the overall resilience to extreme weather events will be higher.

However, a review of the scientific literature reveals that the method of choice is not GE [genetic engineering], but traditional and modern conventional breeding techniques, including marker assisted selection (MAS) [that uses scientific knowledge to speed up breeding but does not result in genetically engineered organisms]. There is considerable scope for breeding a large number of stress traits through the use of traditional varieties. These stress traits are generally regulated by multiple genes, which in turn are tightly controlled by complex interactions between genes, and between the plant and its environment. MAS facilitates the selection of conventional crosses with traits associated with multiple genes, including their as of yet unknown regulatory systems. By contrast, genetic engineering can only crudely insert a single or a few gene(s) without any control over regulatory mechanisms.

In recent years, MAS has yielded breeding successes, including some plants with traits that might be relevant for climate change resilience, such as drought-, heat- or cold-resistant plants. However, it should be emphasised that none of these varieties alone will be able to contribute to food security in a changing climate. For erratic weather with rapid sequences of droughts, floods, storms and heat waves, only a mixed cropping system using a range of crops and varieties can provide the necessary diversity and resilience.

No stress-tolerant GE plants have ever been proven to work under real-world conditions.

Some remarkable MAS successes:

- Rice tolerant to unpredictable floods. Rice production can be subject to stresses such as seasonal flooding, which can be unpredictable and can damage young rice plants. Through genetic mapping, researchers identified a DNA segment containing a gene that makes rice tolerant to prolonged submergence in water. Using MAS, they successfully bred this trait into local and hybrid varieties. This allows the breeding of new varieties resilient to the erratic flooding that may occur as weather patterns become less predictable.

- One expected effect of climate change is the spread of disease. A new strain of wheat stem rust (Ug99), a fungus that can devastate wheat crops, is spreading across Africa. Most cultivated wheat varieties are susceptible to this virulent strain and efforts are under way to develop resistant wheat using MAS. The technique was chosen over GE due to MAS's ability to assist the breeding of complex traits. The breeding programme will use wheat's genetic diversity to find resistance genes that can be bred into high-yielding varieties. This shows the importance of preserving the genetic diversity of crops, which are at risk because modern intensive agriculture relies on very few varieties.

Even Monsanto, the global genetic engineering giant, features this breeding technique in its R&D [research and development] brochures and states under the heading 'Marker Assisted Breeding': "Today, the use of breakthrough technology has reinvented plant breeding so we can more than double the rate of 'genetic gain' in seeds—the improvement in important characteristics such as yield and tolerance to environmental stress."

These examples are evidence that it is possible to transfer plants' complex traits, including their regulatory systems, to commercial varieties using traditional breeding techniques assisted by genetic markers. In contrast to this, GE plants have so far failed to deliver on any of the decade-old promises on stress tolerance. Instead, current GE varieties are particularly susceptible to extreme weather.

The Limits of Genetic Engineering

So far, GE crops are restricted to a few traits that were developed some 20 years ago: herbicide and insect resistance. No stress-tolerant GE plants have ever been proven to work under real-world conditions. The performance of existing GE varieties under climate stress is so far sobering:

- Extreme temperature fluctuations caused crop losses in Bt cotton in China. Researchers investigating the disaster said high temperatures (37 C) [98.6 F] were most probably responsible for causing a drop in Bt concentrations in leaves. Other researchers found that temperature changes, especially a cool period early on in the growing season, caused a reduction in the insect toxicity of Bt.

- GE herbicide-resistant soybeans suffered unexpected losses in the US during very hot spring weather in 1998. Roundup Ready soybeans performed significantly worse than conventional varieties under conditions of heat stress. The GE soybean stems were more brittle and split more easily, thus allowing infection to enter.

- Herbicide-tolerant GE soybeans currently on the market have been reported to have decreased yields of up to 10 percent compared to traditional varieties. Massive herbicide use in conjunction with these GE plants has already led to an increase in tolerant weed populations. For example, 34 cases of glyphosate resistance in nine species have been documented in the US since 2000. Now it is recommended farmers have to spray stronger formulas of herbicides, and mixtures of herbicides adding to costs.

Even if GE might be able to deliver a heat-tolerant plant in 10 or 20 years, what would happen to the plant under extreme cold conditions, unseasonable rain or drought? A single gene does not provide protection against a multitude of conditions.

Currently, most GE stress-tolerant plants in the pipeline use a rather crude approach of over-expressing a single gene throughout the plant's life cycle. This approach is no match for the whole genome network that controls gene expression in natural plants, where genes are switched on and off and moderated throughout the plant's lifetime. By contrast, the inserted gene in the GE plant is on all the time, in all parts of the plant, with no other control. It is like an air conditioner always running at full speed—which could prove deadly in winter.

A one-sided focus on GE plants contradicts all scientific findings on climate change adaptation in agriculture and is a long-term threat to global food security.

In summary, GE plants:

- Will provide no security against extreme weather changes. In a best case scenario, they may be resistant to a single stress, such as heat or drought, but not to the expected rapid and radical weather changes;

- Will lack any sophisticated regulation of the inserted gene and thus cannot respond to changing challenges;

- Because of their higher price, they will most likely be planted in monocultures, which have the highest risk of failing in changeable and extreme weather.

Given genetic engineering's limitations and our limited knowledge about plants' regulated response to environmental stress, unregulated single-trait GE crops are a threat to food security in a changing climate. The prospect of large monocultures of GE plants failing completely under unforeseen weather events is a recipe for disaster.

Biodiverse Farming
Is an Effective Strategy

Biodiverse farming is a proven, effective strategy to adapt to climate change. Through it we can create farms that are able to maintain and increase food production in the face of increasingly unpredictable conditions. In contrast, GE has inherent shortcomings pertaining to plant-environment interactions and complex gene regulations that make it unlikely to address climate change either reliably or in the long term. This conclusion is also reflected in the recent IAASTD [International Assessment of Agricultural Knowledge, Science and Technology for Development] report, which considered GE crops to be irrelevant to achieving the Millennium Development Goals and to eradicating hunger.

Agriculture will not only be negatively affected by climate change, it is a substantial contributor to greenhouse gas emissions. By reducing agriculture's greenhouse gas emissions and by using farming techniques that increase soil carbon, farming itself can contribute to mitigating climate change. In fact, many biodiverse farming systems are both mitigation and adaptation strategies, as they increase soil carbon and use cropping systems that are more resilient to extreme weather.

In order to increase our food security in a changing climate, policy makers need to follow the IAASTD's recommendations and invest more in agricultural R&D that is geared towards modern, effective, biodiverse farming. A one-sided focus on GE plants contradicts all scientific findings on climate change adaptation in agriculture and is a long-term threat to global food security.

Widespread Local Extinctions in Tropical Forest "Remnants"

Space Daily

Space Daily is a science news website. In the following viewpoint, the author reports that deforestation has impacted the tropical forests in eastern Brazil. According to the author, this has resulted in extinctions of mammals throughout the South American country. The author contends that the remaining original forests need to be protected from outside interference.

As you read, consider the following questions:

1. What are some detrimental factors the author names that impact the forest cover?
2. According to the author, about how much of the original Atlantic Forest cover has been converted?
3. What does Dr. Canale recommend implementing to help rare species?

The small fragments of tropical forests left behind after deforestation are suffering extensive species extinction, according to new research led by the University of East Anglia (UEA). Publishing in the journal *PLoS ONE*, the researchers

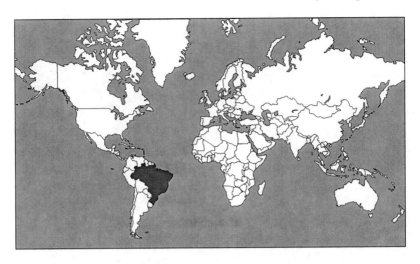

carried out a comprehensive assessment to estimate the long-term impact of forest fragmentation and hunting on tropical biodiversity in Brazil.

They studied the Atlantic Forest of eastern Brazil, including the region's largest and least disturbed old-growth forest remnants, and found that remaining habitat fragments had been virtually emptied of their forest wildlife.

White-lipped peccaries were completely wiped out, while jaguars, lowland tapirs, woolly spider monkeys and giant ant-eaters were virtually extinct. Defaunation even extended to forest remnants with relatively intact canopy structures.

"We uncovered a staggering process of local extinctions of mid-sized and large mammals."

Widespread agricultural expansion has transformed the world's tropical forests, leaving few remaining blocks of primary forests unaltered by humans. There have been scattered reports of large mammal extinctions throughout Brazil, but the conservation value of a rapidly growing number of small forest remnants in highly fragmented tropical forest landscapes has been hotly debated.

105

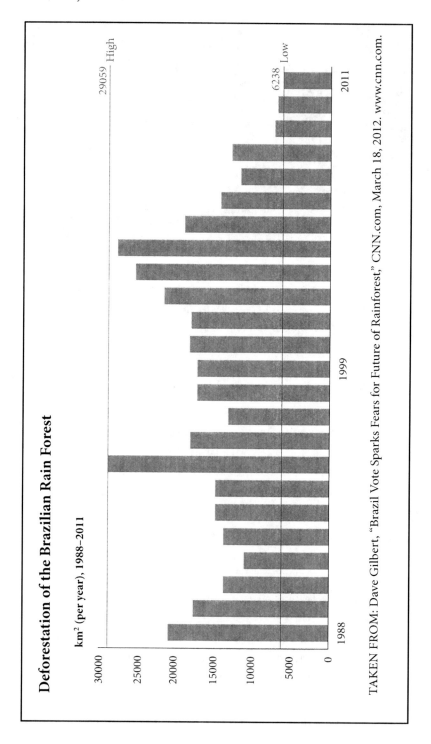

Deforestation of the Brazilian Rain Forest

km² (per year), 1988–2011

29059 High

6238 Low

30000
25000
20000
15000
10000
5000
0

1988

1999

2011

TAKEN FROM: Dave Gilbert, "Brazil Vote Sparks Fears for Future of Rainforest," CNN.com, March 18, 2012. www.cnn.com.

Senior author Prof Carlos Peres, of UEA's School of Environmental Sciences, said: "You might expect forest fragments with a relatively intact canopy structure to still support high levels of biodiversity. Our study demonstrates that this is rarely the case, unless these fragments are strictly protected from hunting pressure.

"There is no substitute for strict protection of remaining forest fragments in biodiversity hot spots like the Brazilian Atlantic Forest. Protection of forest cover alone is not enough to sustain tropical forest species, as overhunting compounds the detrimental effects of small habitat area and isolation."

Drawing on information from wildlife surveys and local interviews conducted at 196 forest fragments spanning a vast region covering 252.670 km^2, Dr Peres worked in partnership with Dr Gustavo Canale of the State University of Mato Grosso (UNEMAT). They investigated the effects of anthropogenic landscape alteration and other impacts, such as hunting, on the survival of large vertebrate species.

The researchers travelled more than 205,000 km by treacherous dirt roads to uncover the largest and least disturbed forest fragments left in this vast region of the Atlantic Forest.

"We uncovered a staggering process of local extinctions of mid-sized and large mammals," said Dr Canale.

Around 90 per cent of the original Atlantic Forest cover (about 1.5 million km^2) has been converted to agriculture, pasture and urban areas, and most of the remaining forest patches are smaller than a football pitch. On average, forest patches retained only four of 18 mammal species surveyed.

This study—the first to document the loss of five large tropical forest mammals from one of the world's most endangered tropical biodiversity hot spots—highlights the critical importance of the few legally protected areas established in the Atlantic Forest.

"We found that the protected areas retained the most species-rich forest fragments in the region," said Dr Canale.

"We therefore recommend the implementation of new strictly protected areas, such as national parks and biological reserves, including forest fragments containing populations of endangered, rare and endemic species, particularly those facing imminent extinctions."

However, many of the existing protected areas are far from secure.

Prof Peres said: "A growing number of reserves are being degraded, downsized, if not entirely degazetted, so holding on to the last remaining large tracts of primary forests will be a crucial part of the conservation mission this century."

With the global population projected to surpass nine billion by 2050, tropical forests will face increasing threats posed by anthropogenic land-use change and overexploitation.

"Human populations are exploding and very few areas remain untouched by the expanding cornucopia of human impacts," said Prof Peres. "It is therefore essential to enforce protection in areas that are nominally protected 'on paper'. The future of tropical forest wildlife depends on it."

In India, Honey Harvesting Is Threatened by Dwindling Biodiversity

Simone Gie

Simone Gie is a writer with the organization Slow Food International, which strives to preserve traditional and regional foods. In the following viewpoint, Gie discusses the practice of jenu, or honey collection, in the Nilgiri mountains of southern India. Collecting the honey from the giant rock bees involves risky descent down steep cliffs. Gie explains that the collection has gone on for generations and is rooted in sustainable practices, as collectors are careful not to take too much at once and to preserve bees for future generations. Gie says that agricultural and economic changes have threatened the practice, but that nongovernmental organizations have worked with the communities to try to ensure the honey collection remains economically viable.

Slow Food is a global, grassroots organization with supporters in 150 countries around the world who are linking the pleasure of good food with a commitment to their community and the environment. A nonprofit member-supported association, Slow Food was founded in 1989 to counter the rise of fast food and fast life, the disappearance of local food traditions, and people's dwindling interest in the food they eat, where it comes from, how it tastes, and how our food choices affect the rest of

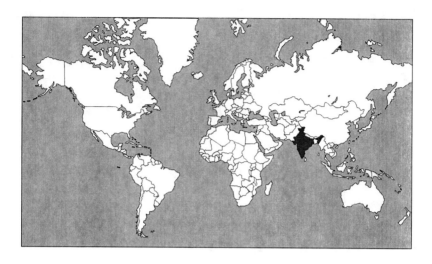

the world. Today, it has more than one hundred thousand mem-
bers joined in fifteen hundred convivia—local chapters—world-
wide, as well as a network of two thousand food communities
who practice small-scale and sustainable production of quality
foods.

As you read, consider the following questions:

1. According to Gie, how can you tell an expert honey
   hunter from an amateur?

2. In what ways does Gie say that honey hunting has
   changed to be more economically viable in modern
   times?

3. What steps do the honey hunters take to conserve the
   bee population, according to Gie?

In the tropical monsoon forests on the slopes of the Nilgiri
mountains in southern India, local tribes risk more than a
sting when they collect the unique wild honey found in this
region. . . . The giant rock bee (*Apis dorsata*) forms its honey-
combs on the high ledges of the mountains' cliffs, requiring
honey hunters to climb down long rope ladders made from
tree bark which take them to combs hundreds of feet in the
air. A loss of balance or a single misstep can be fatal.

Jenu: Hunting Honey Is a Serious Business

Not surprisingly, the business of collecting honey, locally known as jenu, is a serious activity in these forests, under-taken by men who start learning from chief honey hunters during their adolescence. In the week leading up to the mis-sion, the honey hunter prepares. He does not eat meat, he doesn't sleep with his wife, he doesn't partake in village life. He stays alone. He works to achieve a state of calm and men-tal readiness for the task that awaits him.

When the day arrives, the honey hunter travels to the cho-sen location with a support team and lowers himself down the cliff, swinging on the ladder and pushing against the rocks with the agility of an acrobat. When he reaches the combs, he burns a bundle of leaves to calm the colony with the smoke while his assistants lower a basket from above. The basket is positioned below the comb and the hunter uses a long spear to cut off a chunk while singing to the bees, telling them that he is just taking a little bit of their honey for his children, and to please not go away.

You can tell an expert honey hunter from an amateur, they say, as he'll descend the cliffs in broad daylight. Only the cou-rageous and experienced will do this. A learner will go at night, avoiding the sight of the depth of the valley below him, the absence of safety gear and the buzzing mist of bees sur-rounding him like a cloud. An expert can also estimate how full a comb is on sight, based on its orientation, thickness and bulge.

"In the past few years, we have seen many instances of people coming back to forest honey gathering, particu-larly youth."

On the trip back to the village, the team may encounter bears, leopards and elephants that inhabit the thick forest. The area is a UNESCO [United Nations Educational, Scientific and

Cultural Organization] biosphere reserve, and one of the richest biodiversity hot spots in the world. On their return, they will play music on bamboo flutes and a small drum. The song the hunters play will be different depending on the success of the mission, and the rest of the village will know how much honey the team was able to harvest, as they hear the approaching tune.

Continuing the Tradition

The Irula and Kurumba tribes have been practicing honey hunting in this way for generations. Rock paintings in the area depicting honey hunters are estimated to date back more than 2,000 years. Jenu was once a valuable commodity in the bartering system between tribes, and still now plays an important part in their diet, cuisine and medicine.

Today, little has changed with the practice, but as the outside world encroaches, the continuation of this ancient tradition is at risk. "The area is suffering deforestation and there has been a shift in the type of agriculture in the surrounding areas, from multi-cropping to mono-crop land use, and an increase in tea cultivation, which means a loss of diversity and a higher use of pesticides and fertilizers that directly affects the bee population," says Robert Leo from the Keystone Foundation, a local NGO [nongovernmental organization] that has been working with the tribes for more than 15 years to ensure the preservation of the activity. "Plus many are wage-earning opportunities in other fields like textiles, government or factories."

When they cut the comb, they conserve the brood portion (the beehive's young) to ensure future generations of bees.

Since the Keystone Foundation began working with the tribes, the collaboration has focused on how to allow this tradition to continue in the context of a modern society. Through

The Slow Food Movement

The Slow Food movement stands in direct opposition to everything that a fast-food meal represents: blandness, uniformity, conformity, the blind worship of science and technology. The McDonald's Corporation has a slogan, One Taste Worldwide, that perfectly encapsulates the stultifying, homogenizing effects of its global empire.... If fast food is the culinary equivalent of a sound bite, then Slow Food is an honest, thorough declaration of intent. Many tastes are better than one, this new movement says.

Critics of Slow Food claim that it is elitist and effete, too expensive for ordinary people, just the latest trend among foodies and gourmands. I would use a different set of adjectives to describe the movement; necessary and long overdue. Slow foods are mainly peasant foods—dishes and ingredients that have been prepared the same way for centuries. They are time-tested. They spring directly from regional cultures and cuisines. They are not effete. Fast food stems from an entirely different sort of mass culture and mass production. It is a recent phenomenon. Although McDonald's has been around for more than half a century, it did not begin to rely on highly processed, frozen meals until the early 1970s. The centralization and industrialization of our food system has largely occurred over the past twenty years. And its huge social costs—the rise in foodborne illnesses, the advent of new pathogens such as *E. coli* ..., antibiotic resistance from the overuse of drugs in animal feed, extensive water pollution from feedlot wastes, and many others—have become apparent only recently.

Eric Schlosser, "Foreword," The Pleasures of Slow Food: Celebrating Authentic Traditions, Flavors, and Recipes. *San Francisco, CA: Chronicle Books, 2002.*

the project, local production centers have been set up where honey hunters drain, filter and package their honey. They now produce a marketable product sold at a fair price on the shelves in the Keystone Foundation's network of 'Green Shops'. The tribes are now also using the beeswax, previously discarded, to make candles and cosmetics. The foundation has additionally introduced hive keeping, so the hunters have a source of income in the honey-hunting off-season. "In the past few years, we have seen many instances of people coming back to forest honey gathering, particularly youth," says Leo. "One of the reasons is that it is becoming economically viable."

The project has also focused on an increase in quality. Previously the tribes were hand-squeezing the comb to extract the honey, which often meant that pollen, dirt or other substances could contaminate the product. Hunters have now begun to cut the comb and let the honey drain through a proper filter, reducing the risk of impurities.

Preserving the Bees

The wild honey collection still practiced by these tribes is evocative of many of the practices carried out by indigenous peoples across the world—remarkable not only for the traditional knowledge and skills possessed by its practitioners, but for its evolution based on sustainability. Over the years, the hunters have come up with several systems to make the practice sustainable. When they cut the comb, they conserve the brood portion (the beehive's young) to ensure future generations of bees. They may only take a few combs from a certain area of the cliff, or completely avoid entire cliffs as they are considered holy. "If there are ten colonies, they will leave two untouched," even in times of hunger, explained Leo. "And if we consider that bees are responsible for pollinating the forest plants, conserving the bees means conserving the forest."

While he is suspended in the air, the honey hunter's bravery goes beyond the nerve he needs to confront the swarms and the risk of falling. He demonstrates courage of another sort: the ability to stop when his basket is half-full if the combs are poor that year, and return home playing the tune of a failed mission, knowing that by taking only what is sustainable, there will be honey again in the years ahead.

Banking Against Doomsday

Economist

The Economist *is a British news and business weekly magazine. In the following viewpoint, the* Economist *reports on the Svalbard Global Seed Vault, sometimes called the Doomsday Vault, managed by Norway in the Arctic. The vault preserves seeds from around the world, serving as a backup for other local seed vaults that are more vulnerable to natural disaster or political turmoil. The* Economist *says that modern agriculture has resulted in a great loss of crop biodiversity, leaving crops vulnerable to disease or extreme weather. The seed bank helps to preserve that crop variety. However, the* Economist *concludes, more variation among crops and in the wild would provide even better insurance against biodiversity loss.*

As you read, consider the following questions:

1. To what events in the Philippines, Iraq, and Afghanistan does the *Economist* refer to show the need for the global seed bank?

2. Why does the *Economist* say that biotech firms cannot be relied upon to look after crop biodiversity?

3. According to the *Economist*, how has West African sorghum demonstrated its adaptability in recent years?

With a heavy clunk, the steel outer doors of the Svalbard Global Seed Vault closed on February 28th, shutting out a howling Arctic gale and entombing a tonne of new arrivals: 25,000 seed samples from America, Colombia, Costa Rica, Tajikistan, Armenia and Syria. For Cary Fowler, the vault's American architect, the Syrian chickpeas and fava beans were especially welcome.

Opened in 2008, the Svalbard vault is a backup for the world's 1,750 seed banks, storehouses of agricultural biodiversity. To illustrate the need for it, the Philippines' national seed bank was destroyed by fire in January, six years after it was damaged by flooding. Those of Afghanistan and Iraq were destroyed in recent wars. Should the conflict in Syria reach that country's richest store, in Aleppo, the damage would now be less. Some 110,000 Syrian seed samples are now in the Svalbard vault, out of around 750,000 samples in all. "When I see this," says Mr Fowler, looking lovingly at his latest consignment, "I just think, 'thank goodness, they're safe.'"

The Svalbard vault is protected by two air locks, at the end of a tunnel sunk 160 metres into the permafrost of Norway's Arctic archipelago, outside the village of Longyearbyen, one of the world's most northerly habitations. It is maintained at a constant temperature of -18°C. This is serious disaster preparedness: If its electricity were cut, Mr Fowler reckons the vault would take two centuries to warm to freezing point. He also enthusiastically points to its concave tunnel head, designed to deflect the force of a missile strike. Such precautions have spawned the facility's nickname: the Doomsday Vault.

India is reckoned to have had over 100,000 varieties of rice a century ago; it now has only a few thousand.

Mr Fowler, who manages it on behalf of Norway's government, an association of Nordic gene banks and an international body, the Global Crop Diversity Trust, reckons the vault contains samples of around two-thirds of the world's stored crop biodiversity. To augment this, he will also soon embark on a project, funded with $50m from Norway, to collect the seeds of many crops' wild ancestors.

A Seedy Business

Most seed banks were created in the 1970s and 1980s, towards the end of a global surge in crop yields, wrought largely through the adoption of hybridised seed varieties, known as the Green Revolution. The idea was born of a realisation that a vast amount of agricultural biodiversity was being lost, as farmers abandoned old seeds, often locally developed over centuries, for the new hybrids.

The extent of the loss, which continues today, is poorly documented. The extinction of nonhuman species is generally better studied than the loss of the genetic material that sustains humanity. Yet, largely on the basis of named crop varieties that are no longer extant, the UN's Food and Agriculture Organization estimates that 75% of crop biodiversity has been lost from the world's fields. India is reckoned to have had over 100,000 varieties of rice a century ago; it now has only a few thousand. America once had around 5,000 apple varieties, and now has a few hundred. Such measures probably underestimate the scale of the losses, because a single traditional seed variety often contains a lot of genetic diversity.

It is hard to quantify how much this matters; but the long-term risks are potentially huge. Agricultural biodiversity is the best hedge against future blights, including pests, diseases and climate change. That is why plant breeders, from poor smallholders to the world's biggest biotech firms, masters of the genetically modified organism (GMO), continuously update their genetic stock, often from obscure sources.

"If we ignore genetic diversity while we develop GMO products, we risk a disease or pest emerging that will wipe those types out," says John Soper, head of crop genetics research at Pioneer Hi-Bred, the seed division of DuPont, a chemicals giant. He says the firm has drawn genetic material from its stock of wild American sunflower seeds three or four times in the past decade, in a bid to make its commercial varieties resistant to broomrape, a parasitic blight of southern Europe. It also has plans to cope with climate change, having recently opened a research outfit in chilly western Canada. It is trying to develop local varieties of maize (corn) and soybean, which are not grown there commercially, but may be as the temperature climbs.

Seed banks are not the only answer to saving crop biodiversity; it also needs conserving in fields.

Yet biotech firms cannot be relied upon to look after crop biodiversity. Their gene banks are too small and too concentrated on a handful of commercial crops. Their urge to make profits is not necessarily aligned with the wider cause of feeding mankind. Hence a recent push to boost national gene banks, of which the Svalbard vault is a product.

It is a heartening display of international co-operation. In the vault's frozen sanctum, North Korean seeds, in neat brown wooden boxes, sit alongside stocks from South Korea—and from Congo, Bangladesh and Peru. In many such developing countries, gene banks are impoverished and badly managed, which is another threat to their stocks. Pondering one of the risks, Mr Fowler warns "a millennium of agricultural activity can disappear one night in a bowl of porridge."

Let Them Wither on the Vine

Yet seed banks are not the only answer to saving crop biodiversity; it also needs conserving in fields. This is because seed banks rarely store varieties of crops that do not produce seeds, including cassava, bananas and many other fruits and berries. They also rarely record local knowledge of their deposits, which can be almost as important as the seeds themselves. Unlike seed banks, moreover, nature is anything but ossified; it is gloriously adaptable. Over the past 15 years in West Africa, for example, populations of traditional sorghum varieties have been observed shortening their growth cycle by two weeks in response to a curtailed rainy season. The best way to harness this adaptability is simply to let nature get on with it.

Farmers' eagerness to jettison their wily old landraces is understandable. Improved varieties of seed are estimated to have boosted yields by 21–43%, independently of fertilisers and other inputs. To conserve crop biodiversity amid the inevitable rush for hybrids, seed banks have an important role. But another solution—as to many climate-related problems—is to make drastic improvements in land-use planning, and then encourage strategically placed farmers to dedicate a small area to traditional crops. Ways of doing this include developing niche markets for their endearingly old-school vegetables and grains or even, as in Nepal, with the national equivalent of a harvest festival. Its government regularly dishes out prizes to those farmers with the most biodiverse land.

Such measures are less glamorous and more troublesome than depositing seeds in an Arctic bunker kindly paid for by Norwegian taxpayers. That is why they are too rarely taken, which is a great shame. If the world did a better job of tending crop biodiversity in its fields, the feared doomsday after which the vault is nicknamed would be even less likely to come.

Periodical and Internet Sources Bibliography

The following articles have been selected to supplement the diverse views presented in this chapter.

Allianz "Biodiversity Benefits: Rice-Fish Farming in China," http://www.knowledge.allianz .com/environment/food_water/?1503 /biodiversity-benefits-rice-fish-farming -in-china.

Muriel Kakani "Preserving the Biodiversity of Wild Bees and Supporting the Traditional Honey Gatherers," HubPages, September 11, 2009. http://muriel kakani.hubpages.com/hub/support-the-honey gatherers.

New York Times "Bees and Biodiversity Linked to Food Shortage," May 19, 2008.

Michael Oppenheimer and David Wilcove "Understanding the Interactions Between Climate Change, Biodiversity, and Agriculture in South Africa," Princeton University, 2008. http://www.princeton.edu/grandchallenges /development/research-highlights/climate -change.

Fred Pearce "The Cerrado: Brazil's Other Biodiverse Region Loses Ground," *Environment 360*, April 14, 2011.

Matthew Rimmer "The Doomsday Vault: Seed Banks, Food Security and Climate Change," *Selected Works of Matthew Rimmer*, 2012. http://works.bepress .com/matthew_rimmer/102.

Scott Stump "'Doomsday Vault' Holds Seeds That Could Save the World," Today.com, March 2, 2012. http://today.msnbc.msn.com/id/46602078 /ns/today-today_news/t/doomsday-vault-holds -seeds-could-save-world/#.UIGQroUZy9g.

CHAPTER 4

Biodiversity and Climate Change

Climate Change Is Reducing Biodiversity in the Arctic Ocean

William Marsden

William Marsden is a journalist and writer for the Montreal Gazette. *In the following viewpoint, he reports on a multinational study of global warming that shows that climate change is reducing biodiversity in the Arctic. Marsden says that global warming is changing ice thickness, weather, and currents, all of which have an effect on the Arctic ecosystem. He also says that, despite this evidence, public support for scientific study of the Arctic in Canada is diminishing, and the Canadian government has cut funding to study the effects of climate change on the region.*

As you read, consider the following questions:

1. How does Marsden say the energy dynamics of the Arctic Ocean are changing?

2. According to scientists, what is the possible effect of more underwater storms and eddies on local fish populations?

3. Why do scientists argue that funding is crucially needed to study the ozone layer in the Arctic?

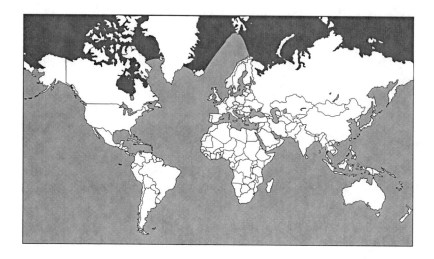

A unique, all-season study of the effects of global warming in the Arctic Ocean shows that climate change is reducing biodiversity and posing "significant challenges to the survival of some of the Arctic's unique marine species."

Warming Changes Ecosystems

The study also shows that climate change is resulting in the increased distribution through the Arctic food chain of contaminants, such as methylmercury.

The $40-million study, which was conducted by 10 scientific teams from 27 countries, spent 2007–2008 studying open water along what are called flaw leads, or breaks in multiyear ice, where they studied how global warming is changing the entire marine ecosystem in the Arctic.

"The Arctic Ocean is definitely changing on a whole lot of different fronts," said Prof. David Barber, of the University of Manitoba.

The study was released Tuesday [in April 2012] at the Polar Year conference in Montreal. The data was gathered aboard the research icebreaker *Amundsen* in the Amundsen Gulf south of Banks Island in the eastern Beaufort Sea.

Scientists explained that with ice coverage and ice thickness reaching record lows over the last decade, the energy dynamics of the Arctic Ocean are changing with profound effects on weather, ocean currents and plant and animal life.

With more solar energy piercing the open waters, ice melt also can affect the carbon exchange between the ocean and the atmosphere. With longer and warmer summers, more carbon dioxide can escape into the atmosphere while in the winter the colder open water can absorb more CO_2. This carbon then can drop with the heavier water to the bottom of the sea and remain there for years.

Prof. Tim Papakyriakou, also of the University of Manitoba, said that scientists are not certain about how much CO_2 is being stored and how much is being released to the atmosphere.

What they did discover is that winter processes can be as important as summer processes in this carbon exchange.

"We still don't know which is dominant," he said.

Scientists also discovered that the open water is becoming a "breeding ground" for underwater storms or eddies. This can bring more nutrients into the Arctic water swelling the populations of local fish, such as Arctic cod—and also attract invasive species.

Government Cutbacks

The Polar Year conference comes at a time when studies indicate that interest in the Arctic among the general population is waning.

Yet scientists found a glimmer of hope in the fact that since February, individual Canadians sent donations totalling $12,000 to help fund a High Arctic research station after the federal government stopped financing it last year.

Prof. James Drummond, of Dalhousie University, said in an interview that the money will help send a student to the Polar Environment Atmospheric Research Laboratory (PEARL) at Eureka, on the western coast of Ellesmere Island.

The *Amundsen* Icebreaker

David Barber, a climatologist from the University of Manitoba, led a remarkable project which sent the Canadian icebreaker *Amundsen* out to the Beaufort Sea from September 2007 until August 2008, right through the winter. It spent much of its time off Cape Bathurst where a giant lead—a long, wide fracture—usually opens up in the ice. No one had ever spent the winter out in the Arctic on a research icebreaker before, so there were plenty of surprises.

"We were expecting ice to form in October, but by the end of November we still had no ice," says Barber. The first part of the explanation is familiar. In the long, hot summer of 2007 the open waters had soaked up heat and were just too warm to freeze quickly. "Climate stations on land were reporting air temperatures of $-20°C$, but over the oceans it was wide open and temperatures were much warmer, around $-2°C$, $-3°C$," says Barber. Then came the surprise. Huge areas of warm air above the ocean fed storms that dumped snow onto the remaining ice. "A meter of fluffy white snow built up and insulated the multilayer pack ice from the cold air so it did not grow as much as it should have done," explains Barber. That left thinner ice to face the summer melt.

Alun Anderson, After the Ice:
Life, Death, and Geopolitics in the New Arctic.
New York: Smithsonian Books, 2009.

Since 2005, the research station had received $1.5 million a year from the Canadian Foundation for Climate and Atmospheric Sciences (CFCAS) to maintain its permanent research station at Eureka.

The federal government created CFCAS in 2000 with a grant of $110 million. The foundation has spent $5.5 million funding the PEARL project. But the Conservative government decided last year not to fund the foundation as of March 1 of this year, which means no more money for PEARL.

Drummond, who heads the PEARL project, said while the amount of money is small, it was nevertheless significant that more than 150 Canadians reacted to the government's decision by sending donations for PEARL to the foundation. Individual donations ranged from $5 to $1,000.

The federal government's decision to stop funding this research came at a critical time for PEARL's research into the ozone layer.

Dawn Conway, executive director of the foundation, said the donations came to the foundation despite the fact CFCAS did not advertise.

The federal government's decision to stop funding this research came at a critical time for PEARL's research into the ozone layer.

Drummond said that last year, the hole in the ozone over the Arctic was larger than it has ever been and it is vital that the world permanently monitors this striking ozone depletion.

The government argues it is creating a new research station at Cambridge Bay, which is about 1,000 kilometres south of Eureka.

"It's like predicting the weather in Montreal by collecting weather data in Georgia," Drummond said.

He said PEARL also is a vital station for the verification of data collected by satellites orbiting over the Arctic. He said unless satellite data on atmospheric science are verified by Earth-based stations, nobody can be sure if the data are accurate. The position of PEARL'S High Arctic station is ideal for satellite verification, he said.

On April 30, PEARL will cease full-time, year-around operations.

Threats Loom for Australia's Outback Biodiversity

Targeted News Service

Targeted News Service (TNS) is a newswire that provides information related to federal government activities. In the following viewpoint, the author explains that Australia's outback has a unique biodiversity that is supported by its groundwater. The author argues that climate change will damage this biodiversity by drying up the water holes that are important to mobile species. The author further notes that water management will be an essential tool in the aid of the outback's organisms.

As you read, consider the following questions:

1. According to the viewpoint, what are the ecological refuges in the outback?
2. What are some species named in the viewpoint that gorges, springs, and riverine water holes support?
3. According to the author, what is the impact of climate change on the groundwater in the outback?

MELBOURNE, Australia, April 24—Monash University issued the following news release:

Biologists have developed a new approach to identify major threats to the aquatic habitats that support freshwater life in drier parts of Australia.

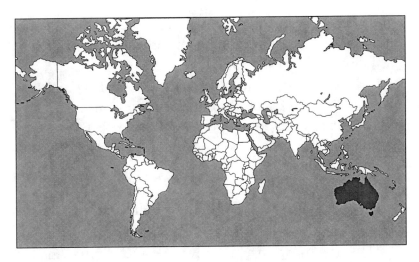

In a study published in the journal *Global Change Biology*, researchers worked on some of Australia's most iconic outback sites, including the central Australian gorges, mound springs and the Coopers Creek, Georgina, and Diamantina River region in western Queensland, to identify the types of habitat that are likely to be vulnerable to climate change and how management may address this.

Seeking to guide conservation planning, researchers Professor Jenny Davis, Dr Alexandra Pavlova, Associate Professor Paul Sunnucks and Dr Ross Thompson, from the Australian Centre for Biodiversity at Monash University, characterised the different types of aquatic habitats in arid regions as either evolutionary refugia or ecological refuges.

Professor Davis said the method enabled them to detail the vulnerabilities of these habitats, and the animal life they support, to a changing climate.

"Look beyond the red dunes, dry plains and rocky outcrops of inland Australia and it is the presence of water, especially groundwater, that sustains rare and unique biodiversity," Professor Davis said.

"Evolutionary refugia are permanent springs, fed by groundwater, that contain relict species from wetter times, in some cases from millions of years ago. These ancient species will become extinct if a spring dries through overpumping of groundwater.

"Ecological refuges are the water holes that fill and flow after flooding rains. These are important for mobile species such as waterbirds and fish. These water holes and the species they support are vulnerable to dams and off-takes that stop beneficial flooding."

The research highlighted the importance of groundwater in a drying and warming world as a buffer for arid springs and water holes against climatic changes.

"The gorges, springs and riverine water holes support many aquatic species, including waterbirds, fish and a wide variety of invertebrates, as well as being a focus for terrestrial birds, reptiles and marsupials," Professor Davis said.

"Managing this water wisely is critical, with adaptive management an important tool for ensuring the future survival of many of the outback's iconic organisms."

"Across all of outback Australia there is an urgent need to manage the threats to inland aquatic biodiversity."

The rivers form one of the last near-natural desert river systems left in the world, transforming from an arid environment as masses of water travel hundreds of kilometres from the Great Dividing Range in Queensland to South Australia's Lake Eyre. Nearby, the mound springs fed by the Great Artesian Basin represent islands of water in a sea of desert and contain unique collections of plants and animals.

The study emphasised the necessity of ensuring that outback industries, including mining, pastoralism and tourism, manage water wisely.

"Unique freshwater ecosystems are experiencing rapid declines in biodiversity due to a range of threats including large-scale irrigation, mining, water pollution and invasive species like mosquito fish," Professor Davis said.

"Across all of outback Australia there is an urgent need to manage the threats to inland aquatic biodiversity and protect the ability of aquatic habitats to cope with changing climates."

The study was commissioned by the Australian government through the National Climate Change Adaptation Research Fund and the National Water Commission.

Climate Change Threatens Jamaica's Biodiversity

Zadie Neufville

Zadie Neufville is a reporter for Inter Press Service (IPS). In the following viewpoint, she reports that Jamaica has an extensive range of species and is an important center for biodiversity. However, she says, development, a lack of focus on preservation, and climate change are threatening the island's plants and wildlife. She says scientists are working to catalogue species and to estimate the possible effects of climate change. Among the dangers from global warming are more intense rainy days, increased hurricanes, and periodic drought, all of which may threaten some of Jamaica's species.

As you read, consider the following questions:

1. What are the Millennium Development Goals, and what does Neufville say Jamaican authorities hope to accomplish by working toward the seventh goal?
2. What does Neufville identify as some of the best-known species on Jamaica?
3. Who rediscovered the Jamaican iguana, and what does that say about Jamaican development, according to Neufville?

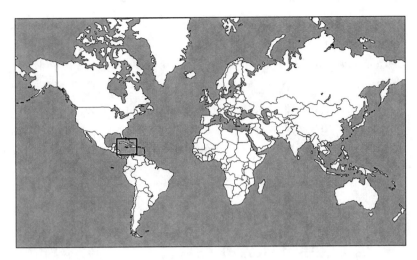

Jamaican authorities are going all out to achieve environ-mental sustainability as one way of minimising the expected impacts of climate change on the local biodiversity.

Climate Change and Disregard for the Ecosystem

There is no up-to-date inventory of the island's flora and fauna, and a shortage of adequate data collection devices, which researchers say are needed to begin climate impact studies and adaptation planning in ecosystems management.

But, by working toward the seventh Millennium Develop-ment Goal (MDG)—a series of development and antipoverty targets agreed by U.N. [United Nations] member states in 2000—authorities hope to establish the principles of sustain-able development across all sectors to reduce environmental degradation, reverse the loss of environmental resources, and significantly reduce the rate of biodiversity loss.

Ecosystems manager at the National Environment and Planning Agency (NEPA) Andrea Donaldson told IPS [Inter Press Service] that while the agency's work on biodiversity is not focused on climate change, they are aware of the likely impacts and continue to implement measures to safeguard the local biological diversity.

The national MDG report has pointed to the country's failures in efforts at pollution controls and the protection of critical ecosystems, and it is these factors that worry scientists the most.

In addition, human activities that result in deforestation, destruction of wetlands and coastal ecosystems, urban sprawl as well as disregard for the natural environment have been identified as some of the most serious threats to biodiversity.

This is the most bio-endemic island in the region. Ranking fifth amongst islands of the world for the number of unique species, Jamaica's biodiversity losses could be immense.

In fact, experts are concerned that disregard for the natural environment could exacerbate the impacts of severe weather. Both the 2010 State of the Environment Report (SOE) and the National Report to the United Nations Framework Convention on Climate Change (UNFCCC) pointed to human activities as significant threats.

"Climate change is likely to further increase the negative impacts" of habitat loss, overexploitation, poor land use and ignorance about the value of natural resources, the SOE reported.

Some experts are already describing changes in coral reefs, forests and coastal wetlands, areas that have been identified as most vulnerable to climate change. It is widely believed that with more than 12 extreme weather events in the last five years, Jamaica is already feeling the effects.

Immense Losses Are Possible

This is the most bio-endemic island in the region. Ranking fifth amongst islands of the world for the number of unique species, Jamaica's biodiversity losses could be immense. There are more than 8,000 recorded species of plants and animals and more than 3,500 marine species here.

Among the island's endemic treasures are 10 species of cacti, seven species of palms and 60 of the 240 species of orchids. There are 31 endemic species of birds, nine species of crabs, 505 species of the 514 varieties of land snails, and 33 of the 43 species of reptiles.

At least four of the 24 species of bats here are endemic; 17 of the 19 species of frogs and about 15 of the 115 species of butterflies.

Among the better-known unique species are the tody, the Jamaican boa, the Jamaican hutia also called the coney and the giant swallowtail butterfly.

The island ranks among the International Union for Conservation of Nature's (IUCN) list of places with the highest number of at-risk mammals, due primarily to the threat to its endemic bats and the coney.

Another of the island's endemic species, the Jamaican iguana, is on the IUCN's Red List of endangered and threatened species. Roughly 200 of the animals survive in the shrinking limestone forests of Hillshire, several miles outside the capital Kingston.

And as the impacts of fewer but more intense rainy days, increased intensity of hurricanes, and periodic drought take their toll, socioeconomic problems are expected to increase the pressure on natural resources.

As the agency charged with safeguarding the island's biological treasures, NEPA said it has spearheaded a number of policies, programmes and legislation to manage and prevent unauthorised exploitation.

Its managers admit, however, that enforcement has been difficult, so like the Forestry Department, NEPA is making the impacted communities its allies. Adaptation funding has enabled both agencies to replant the forests and coastal wetlands. At the same time, they are working with fishers, farmers and others whose livelihoods depend on the natural ecosystems to find other income-generating opportunities.

The multi-sector, multi-donor climate change adaptation and disaster mitigation project is funded by the European Union. It also complements NEPA's efforts to assign economic value to the ecosystem and improve data collection to inform climate change planning.

"We are trying to install data loggers to collect information on sea water surface temperature among other things," Donaldson noted. "While we do regular reef checks, I can't say as a fact that any changes we see are from climate change."

NEPA's data loggers should provide the Jamaica Clearing-House Mechanism (CHM) with information that would be useful in studying the impact of climate change on its vast though outdated databases of plants and animals, biologist Keron Campbell said.

"We are updating the baseline data, the inventories of plant and animal species and this is needed to track any changes," Campbell told IPS, noting that data loggers, along with ongoing field studies and temperature information from the meteorological service, will provide valuable data for adaptation planning.

Jamaica's Natural History Museum, which houses the CHM, holds 110,000 zoological specimens and a herbarium of 130,000 plant specimens dating back to the 1870s. The CHM is part of an international network and is the result of Jamaica's commitment under the U.N. Convention on Biological Diversity.

Donaldson also pointed to charcoal burning, farming, solid waste disposal in freshwater sources and coastal areas, and improper fishing methods including the use of chemicals as some of the most prevalent and worrying factors that impact biodiversity.

Encroaching Development

The SOE reported that scientists are also seeing changes in the Portland Bight [Protected Area], the island's largest nature reserve. It is also the only known habitat of the Jamaican iguana.

"Some of the best birding trails are being replaced by houses."

Dr. Byron Wilson, head of the University of the West Indies iguana programme, noted that the continued survival of the iguana is due primarily to the remoteness of its habitat. Efforts to build a colony on Goat Island just off the coast failed, he said, making the Hellshire Hills one of the world's most important natural habitats.

But development is now making the area more accessible. It was a pig hunter who rediscovered the iguana that had been thought extinct for more than 30 years.

NEPA's wildlife specialist Ricardo Miller noted that the most significant changes during the annual game birds survey is the rate of development.

"I have had to change my sampling routes due to developmental changes. Some of the best birding trails are being replaced by houses," he said.

Jamaica's climate change preparations began in 1997 with Caribbean Planning for Adaptation to Climate Change (CPACC) under CARICOM (the regional Caribbean Community bloc). The programme initiated, among other things, the design strategies and databases for climate change adaptation in a number of areas.

If the science is correct, Donaldson said, climate change will result in the inundation of coastal areas, loss of habitat and the dying off of some species. Others, she added, may very well adapt.

International Programs Can Help Indonesia Fight Climate Change and Biodiversity Loss

Celia A. Harvey, Jonah Busch, and Muhammad Farid

Celia A. Harvey is a vice president, Jonah Busch is an economist, and Muhammad Farid is a climate change specialist with Conservation International. In the following viewpoint, they argue that deforestation is a prime driver of biodiversity loss in Indonesia. Deforestation also contributes to carbon dioxide emissions, which fuel climate change. The authors contend that Indonesia should take part in the United Nations Reducing Emissions from Deforestation and Forest Degradation program (REDD+), a policy mechanism whereby developed countries provide developing countries with incentives to reduce emissions and slow deforestation. The authors conclude that if Indonesia can use REDD+ to slow deforestation in order to reduce greenhouse gas emissions, biodiversity will benefit greatly as well.

As you read, consider the following questions:

1. Each year, how much CO_2 is released due to deforestation, and for what percentage of greenhouse gas emissions does this account, according to the authors?

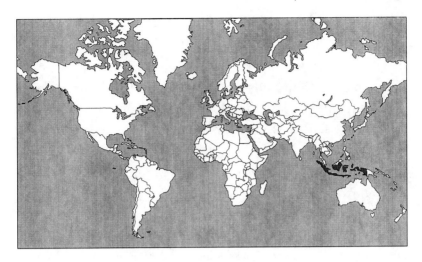

2. What three reasons do the authors give for believing that REDD+ will preserve biodiversity as well as reduce greenhouse emissions?

3. Why do the authors say REDD+ alone is not enough to solve either the climate change or biodiversity crisis?

The international community is currently tackling two urgent global problems: the rapid increase in climate change and the ongoing loss of biodiversity. Two weeks ago [October 2010], delegates from around the world gathered in Nagoya, Japan, to discuss the failure of countries to meet their 2010 biodiversity targets and to propose new targets for reducing further biodiversity loss. And, at the end of this month, country delegates will convene in Cancun, Mexico, to continue the ongoing climate negotiations and seek solutions to the climate crisis.

REDD+ Provides Incentives

One topic that is critical is how to deal with deforestation and degradation of the world's tropical forests.

Each year, roughly 13 million hectares of forests are cleared globally, resulting in the emission of around 4.4 billion tons of

CO_2, or roughly 15 percent of the greenhouse gas emissions responsible for climate change.

This deforestation also leads to the loss of hundreds—or perhaps even thousands—of plant and animal species, and negatively impacts local and indigenous communities who depend on these forests for their livelihoods.

In Indonesia alone, it is estimated that roughly 1 million hectares of forests are lost each year, resulting in the annual emission of more than a billion tons of CO_2, and negatively impacting Indonesia's biodiversity. Indonesia has a very rich biodiversity, including at least 58 amphibian species, 182 bird species and 141 mammal species that are endemic to its forests and are found nowhere else on earth.

REDD+ [Reducing Emissions from Deforestation and Forest Degradation] offers an opportunity to tackle both of these problems simultaneously. REDD+ is an international policy mechanism in which developed countries provide incentives to developing countries to reduce emissions from deforestation and degradation, and to enhance carbon sequestration [the capture and long-term storage of carbon] through forest conservation, carbon stock enhancement and sustainable management.

For Indonesia, REDD+ is an unprecedented opportunity to conserve its remaining forests, significantly reduce its greenhouse gas emissions and earn revenue in support of sustainable development. It is also a unique opportunity to conserve forest habitat for the country's remarkable biodiversity.

Reducing Greenhouse Gases Will Preserve Biodiversity

Although the REDD+ mechanism is designed primarily to reduce greenhouse gas emissions from the forest sector, there are several reasons why it is also likely to provide unprecedented benefits for biodiversity.

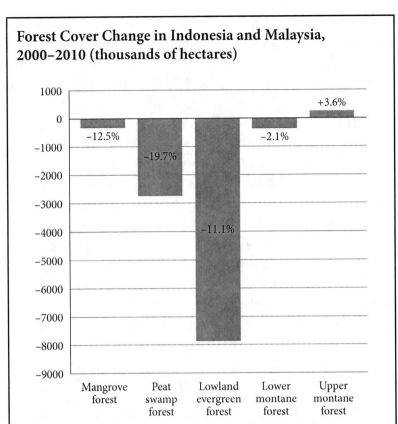

Forest Cover Change in Indonesia and Malaysia, 2000–2010 (thousands of hectares)

TAKEN FROM: Rhett Butler, "Charts: Deforestation in Indonesia and Malaysia, 2000–2010," Mongabay.com, July 15, 2012. www.mongabay.com.

First, for REDD+ to be successful, policy makers will need to find ways to address the many drivers of deforestation and degradation of tropical forests. Most of these drivers of deforestation are also the key threats to biodiversity conservation.

Second, the approaches that policy makers will use to conserve and sustainably manage forests will likely build on approaches already developed and implemented by the conservation community. These key approaches include payments to local communities and jurisdictions that conserve forest, the expansion of the protected area system, the improved management of existing protected areas, recognition of indigenous communities and community-managed areas, prevention of fires, as well as the use of agroforestry systems and agricultural intensification on degraded land to reduce pressure on remaining forests.

Third, both REDD+ and biodiversity conservation are dependent on good governance. Under REDD+, governments will need to strengthen their forest governance, enhance their capacity to monitor forest cover and illegal logging, and develop clear legal and financial frameworks and law enforcement to protect remaining forests.

In addition, they will need to clarify land tenure issues and carbon rights. All of the steps towards improving forest governance will not only help ensure that REDD+ conserves forests and reduces greenhouse gas emissions, but also benefits the biodiversity that relies upon these forests.

If REDD+ is well designed and appropriately implemented, it would be a giant and historic step forward towards solving both the climate and biodiversity crises.

Finally, the success of both REDD+ and biodiversity conservation efforts will depend on active participation and support of local stakeholders. If local communities and stakeholders are well informed and supportive of efforts to reduce deforestation and degradation and actively involved in decision making and implementation of REDD+, it is more likely that forests will be conserved over the long term, providing both mitigation and biodiversity benefits.

Of course, REDD+ on its own is not enough to solve either the climate change or biodiversity crisis. In order to tackle climate change, additional mitigation activities such as reducing fossil fuel use, using renewable energy and promoting energy efficiency through development of a low carbon development strategy are needed.

To achieve biodiversity conservation, additional conservation measures will be needed in non-forest ecosystems and in areas that may have little mitigation potential but are of important conservation value.

However, if REDD+ is well designed and appropriately implemented, it would be a giant and historic step forward towards solving both the climate and biodiversity crises. With its vast (but rapidly disappearing) forests and extraordinary biodiversity, Indonesia is in a unique position to provide global leadership in ensuring REDD+ delivers both climate mitigation and biodiversity benefits.

Biodiversity Loss Is as Much of an Ecological Threat as Climate Change

National Science Foundation

The National Science Foundation (NSF) is an independent federal agency that supports research and education in science and engineering. In the following viewpoint, NSF reports on an international study that investigated the ecological effects of biodiversity loss. The study concluded that loss of species can have a major effect on plant growth and ecological health. This effect is comparable to that of other major environmental stressors, such as climate change or pollution. The study, therefore, concluded that scientists and policy makers need to pay more attention to the possible ecological effects of biodiversity loss.

As you read, consider the following questions:

1. To what does the viewpoint attribute the very high rates of modern extinction?
2. What effects did the study find in cases where species loss fell within 1 to 20 percent of plant species?
3. What does J. Emmett Duffy say is the biggest challenge for environmental scientists looking forward?

"Ecosystem Effects of Biodiversity Loss Rival Climate Change and Pollution," National Science Foundation, May 2, 2012. Courtesy: National Science Foundation.

Loss of biodiversity appears to affect ecosystems as much as climate change, pollution and other major forms of environmental stress, according to results of a new study by an international research team.

Stronger Protections Needed

The study is the first comprehensive effort to directly compare the effects of biological diversity loss to the anticipated effects of a host of other human-caused environmental changes.

The results, published in this week's [May 2012] issue of the journal *Nature*, highlight the need for stronger local, national and international efforts to protect biodiversity and the benefits it provides, according to the researchers, who are based at nine institutions in the United States, Canada and Sweden.

"This analysis establishes that reduced biodiversity affects ecosystems at levels comparable to those of global warming and air pollution," said Henry Gholz, program director in the National Science Foundation's Division of Environmental Biology, which funded the research directly and through the National Center for Ecological Analysis and Synthesis.

"Some people have assumed that biodiversity effects are relatively minor compared to other environmental stressors," said biologist David Hooper of Western Washington University, the lead author of the paper.

"Our results show that future loss of species has the potential to reduce plant production just as much as global warming and pollution."

Studies over the last two decades demonstrated that more biologically diverse ecosystems are more productive.

As a result, there has been growing concern that the very high rates of modern extinctions—due to habitat loss, over-harvesting and other human-caused environmental changes—could reduce nature's ability to provide goods and services such as food, clean water and a stable climate.

Until now, it's been unclear how biodiversity losses stack up against other human-caused environmental changes that affect ecosystem health and productivity.

Major Effects

"Loss of biological diversity due to species extinctions is going to have major effects on our planet, and we need to prepare ourselves to deal with them," said ecologist Bradley Cardinale of the University of Michigan, one of the paper's coauthors. "These extinctions may well rank as one of the top five drivers of global change."

In the study, Hooper, Cardinale and colleagues combined data from a large number of published studies to compare how various global environmental stressors affect two processes important in ecosystems: plant growth and the decomposition of dead plants by bacteria and fungi.

The study involved the construction of a database drawn from 192 peer-reviewed publications about experiments that manipulated species richness and examined their effect on ecosystem processes.

At higher levels of extinction . . . , the effects of species loss ranked with those of many other major drivers of environmental change, such as ozone pollution, acid deposition on forests and nutrient pollution.

This global synthesis found that in areas where local species loss during this century falls within the lower range of projections (losses of 1 to 20 percent of plant species), negligible effects on ecosystem plant growth will result, and changes in species richness will rank low relative to the effects projected for other environmental changes.

In ecosystems where species losses fall within intermediate projections of 21 to 40 percent of species, however, species loss is expected to reduce plant growth by 5 to 10 percent.

The effect is comparable to the expected effects of climate warming and increased ultraviolet radiation due to stratospheric ozone loss.

At higher levels of extinction (41 to 60 percent of species), the effects of species loss ranked with those of many other major drivers of environmental change, such as ozone pollution, acid deposition on forests and nutrient pollution.

"Within the range of expected species losses, we saw average declines in plant growth that were as large as changes in experiments simulating several other major environmental changes caused by humans," Hooper said.

"Several of us working on this study were surprised by the comparative strength of those effects."

The strength of the observed biodiversity effects suggests that policy makers searching for solutions to other pressing environmental problems should be aware of potential adverse effects on biodiversity as well.

Still to be determined is how diversity loss and other large-scale environmental changes will interact to alter ecosystems.

"The biggest challenge looking forward is to predict the combined effects of these environmental challenges to natural ecosystems and to society," said J. Emmett Duffy of the Virginia Institute of Marine Science, a coauthor of the paper.

Periodical and Internet Sources Bibliography

The following articles have been selected to supplement the diverse views presented in this chapter.

Bob Beale
"Biodiversity and Climate Change—From Bad to Worse," Phys.org, December 8, 2011.

Desmond Brown
"Climate Change Affecting Caribbean Hotel Industry," Caribbean360, October 18, 2012. http://www.caribbean360.com/index.php /news/st_kitts_nevis_news/625175.html #axzz291y7Qp1f.

Conservation International
"REDD+: A Win-Win for Climate and Biodiversity," November 29, 2010. http://www.conservation.org/newsroom /pressreleases/Pages/REDDplus_a_win-win _for_climate_biodiversity.aspx.

Energy Korea
"Why Indonesia's Biodiversity Is at the Front Line of the Fight Against Climate Change," August 17, 2012. http://energy.korea.com /archives/33556.

International Arctic Science Committee
"Effects of Climate Change on the Biodiversity of the Arctic," *Encyclopedia of Earth*, May 7, 2012. http://www.eoearth.org/article /Effects_of_climate_change_on_the _biodiversity_of_the_Arctic.

Nicky Phillips
"Protecting Biodiversity Would Limit Damage," *Sydney Morning Herald*, December 12, 2011.

Tara Thean
"Biodiversity Has Increased During Earth's Warm Periods. But Climate Change Isn't Off the Hook," *Time*, September 4, 2012.

Petre Williams-Raynor
"'Jamaica's Biodiversity Threatened,'" *Jamaica Observer*, July 27, 2010.

For Further Discussion

Chapter 1

1. Based on the viewpoints in this chapter, what is the effect of business on biodiversity? Does it help preserve it or tend to destroy it? Defend your answer using specific examples from the viewpoints in the chapter.

2. How do political factors influence development and biodiversity? Use specific examples from the viewpoints in this chapter.

Chapter 2

1. Can an increase in wildlife populations ever *threaten* biodiversity? Use specific examples from the viewpoints in this chapter to support your answer.

2. How can human factors have an effect on biodiversity in a given area? Use specific examples from the viewpoints in this chapter to formulate your answer.

Chapter 3

1. Is agriculture a threat to biodiversity? Explain your answer using evidence from the viewpoints in this chapter.

2. Imagine that you had invented a new variety of super grain that was resistant to drought, heat, cold, and pests, and that had a very high yield. Should your new super grain replace all grains everywhere? Why or why not? Use evidence from the viewpoints in this chapter to support your answer.

Chapter 4

1. William Marsden talks about how global warming is damaging biodiversity in the Arctic. Is warming only a threat to biodiversity in cold climates? Why or why not? Use examples from the viewpoints in this chapter to support your answer.

Organizations to Contact

The editors have compiled the following list of organizations concerned with the issues debated in this book. The descriptions are derived from materials provided by the organizations. All have publications or information available for interested readers. The list was compiled on the date of publication of the present volume; the information provided here may change. Be aware that many organizations take several weeks or longer to respond to inquiries, so allow as much time as possible.

American Council on Science and Health (ACSH)

1995 Broadway, Suite 202, New York, NY   10023-5882
(212) 362-7044 • fax: (212) 362-4919
e-mail: acsh@acsh.org
website: www.acsh.org

The American Council on Science and Health (ACSH) is a consumer education consortium concerned with environmental and health-related issues. The council publishes the quarterly *Priorities*, position papers, and articles such as "Why Biodiversity Is a Public Health Issue" and "Problems with the Cartagena Protocol," which are available on its website.

Cato Institute

1000 Massachusetts Avenue NW
Washington, DC   20001-5403
(202) 842-0200 • fax: (202) 842-3490
e-mail: cato@cato.org
website: www.cato.org

The Cato Institute is a libertarian public policy research foundation that aims to limit the role of government and protect civil liberties. In addition to a wide range of journals and newsletters, Cato publishes books, including *Meltdown: The Predictable Distortion of Global Warming by Scientists, Politi-*

cians, and the Media. Publications offered on its website include recent issues of the bimonthly *Cato Policy Report*, the quarterly journal *Regulation*, policy studies, and opinions and commentary.

Conservation International
2011 Crystal Drive, Suite 500, Arlington, VA   22202
(703) 341-2400
website: www.conservation.org

Conservation International's goal is to promote biological research and work with national governments and businesses to protect biodiversity hot spots worldwide. On its website, the organization publishes fact sheets that explain its values, mission, and strategies, as well as news and reports of its successes.

Environment Canada
Inquiry Center, 10 Wellington, 23rd Floor
Gatineau   QC K1A 0H3
   Canada
(819) 997-2800 • fax: (819) 994-1412
e-mail: enviroinfo@ec.gc.ca
website: www.ec.gc.ca

Environment Canada is a department of the Canadian government. Its goal is the achievement of sustainable development in Canada through conservation and environmental protection. The department publishes reports, fact sheets, news, and speeches, many of which are available on its website.

Friends of the Earth International (FOEI)
PO Box 19199, Amsterdam   1000 GD
   The Netherlands
31 20 622 1369 • fax: 31 20 639 2181
website: www.foei.org

Friends of the Earth International (FOEI) is a grassroots environmental network. Its member organizations campaign worldwide for food sovereignty, economic justice, and biodiversity, among other environmental and social justice issues. Its website includes news releases, reports, and numerous other publications and resources about topics such as biodiversity and the drawbacks of genetically modified crops.

Greenpeace USA

702 H Street NW, Suite 300, Washington, DC   20001
(800) 722-6995 • fax: (202) 462-4507
e-mail: info@wdc.greenpeace.org
website: www.greenpeaceusa.org

Greenpeace USA opposes nuclear energy and the use of toxic chemicals and supports ocean and wildlife preservation. It uses controversial direct-action techniques and strives for media coverage of its actions in an effort to educate the public. It publishes the quarterly magazine *Greenpeace* as well as the books *Coastline* and *The Greenpeace Book on Antarctica*. On its website, Greenpeace publishes fact sheets, reports such as "Food Security and Climate Change: The Answer Is Biodiversity," and articles such as "How Should We Protect Biodiversity and Our Climate?"

Institute of Science in Society (ISIS)

29 Tytherton Road, London   N19 4PZ
(0) 1908 696101
e-mail: jules@i-sis.org.uk
website: www.i-sis.org.uk

The Institute of Science in Society (ISIS) is a not-for-profit organization dedicated to providing critical and accessible scientific information to the public and to promoting social accountability and ecological sustainability in science. ISIS provides scientific advice to the Third World Network, a nongovernmental organization based in Penang, Malaysia. It also runs training programs about genetic engineering in developing countries and elsewhere, and it produces scientific papers on topics such as biodiversity. ISIS publishes the quarterly magazine *Science in Society* as well as other publications and reports, all available through its website.

Intergovernmental Panel on Climate Change (IPCC)

IPCC Secretariat C/O World Meteorological Organization
7bis Avenue de la Paix, C.P. 2300, Geneva 2   CH-1211
  Switzerland
+41-22-730-8208 • fax: +41-22-730-8025
e-mail: IPCC-Sec@wmo.int
website: www.ipcc.ch

The World Meteorological Organization (WMO) and the
United Nations Environment Programme (UNEP) established
the Intergovernmental Panel on Climate Change (IPCC) in
1988. The role of the IPCC is to assess information relevant to
understanding the scientific basis of risk of human-induced
climate change, its potential impacts, and options for adaptation and mitigation. The IPCC website includes press releases,
global climate change reports, links, and publications available
for free download.

Natural Capital Project

371 Serra Mall, Stanford University
Stanford, CA   94305-5020
(650) 725-1783 • fax: (650) 723-5920
e-mail: invest@naturalcapitalproject.org
website: www.naturalcapitalproject.org

The Natural Capital Project is a joint venture of Stanford University, the Nature Conservancy, and the World Wildlife Fund
that explores ecosystem services and economy incentives for
preserving biodiversity. It develops tools to quantify the value
of natural capital to integrate scientific and economic understanding of natural assets into land-use and investment decisions. Its website provides information on books by project
members, such as *The New Economy of Nature: The Quest to
Make Conservation Profitable,* and many articles by project
members, including "Using Science to Assign Value to Nature"
and "When Agendas Collide: Human Welfare and Biological
Conservation."

Slow Food USA

68 Summit Street, 2B, Brooklyn, NY   11231

(718) 260-8000 • fax: (718) 260-8068

e-mail: membership@slowfoodusa.org

website: www.slowfoodusa.org

Slow Food USA is an organization and a grassroots movement that promotes traditional foods and links the pleasure of eating to a commitment to community and the environment. Its website includes back issues of its magazine the *Snail*, blog posts, and articles about food, agriculture, biodiversity, and other environmental topics.

World Resources Institute (WRI)

10 G Street NE, Suite 800, Washington, DC   20002

(202) 729-7600 • fax: (202) 729-7610

website: www.wri.org

The World Resources Institute (WRI) conducts research on ecosystem threats and works with indigenous communities to balance human and wildlife needs. Its website provides links to its four primary areas of study: climate protection, governance, markets and enterprise, and people and ecosystems. WRI provides fact sheets, working papers, and reports on its website, including "Biodiversity Loss: Cascade Effects" and "Measuring Nature's Benefits: A Preliminary Roadmap for Improving Ecosystem Service Indicators."

Bibliography of Books

Andrew Blackwell *Visit Sunny Chernobyl: And Other Adventures in the World's Most Polluted Places.* New York: Rodale Books, 2012.

Eric Chivian and Aaron Bernstein, eds. *Sustaining Life: How Human Health Depends on Biodiversity.* New York: Oxford University Press, 2008.

Sneed B. Collard III *Science Warriors: The Battle Against Invasive Species.* New York: Houghton Mifflin, 2008.

Sofia A. Contreras, eds. *Effects of Climate Change on Aquatic Invasive Species.* New York: Nova Science Publishers, 2010.

Francisco Dallmeier et al., eds. *Climate Change, Biodiversity and Sustainability in the Americas: Impacts and Adaptations.* Washington, DC: Smithsonian Institution Scholarly Press, 2010.

A. Damodaran *Encircling the Seamless: India, Climate Change, and the Global Commons.* New York: Oxford University Press, 2010.

Tui de Roy *Galápagos: Preserving Darwin's Legacy.* Buffalo, NY: Firefly, 2009.

Akiko Domoto et al., eds. *A Threat to Life: The Impact of Climate Change on Biodiversity.* Gland, Switzerland: IUCN, 2000.

Elizabeth C. Economy — *The River Runs Black: The Environmental Challenge to China's Future.* 2nd ed. Ithaca, NY: Cornell University Press, 2010.

Paul Gepts et al., eds. — *Biodiversity in Agriculture: Domestication, Evolution, and Sustainability.* New York: Cambridge University Press, 2012.

R.E. Hester and R.M. Harrison, eds. — *Biodiversity Under Threat.* Cambridge, United Kingdom: Royal Society of Chemistry, 2007.

Ray Hilborn with Ulrike Hilborn — *Overfishing: What Everyone Needs to Know.* New York: Oxford University Press, 2012.

Pushpam Kumar, ed. — *The Economics of Ecosystems and Biodiversity: Ecological and Economic Foundations.* New York: Routledge, 2012.

Thomas E. Lovejoy and Lee Hannah, eds. — *Climate Change and Biodiversity.* New Haven, CT: Yale University Press, 2005.

Celia Lowe — *Wild Profusion: Biodiversity Conservation in an Indonesian Archipelago.* Princeton, NJ: Princeton University Press, 2006.

Donald S. Maier — *What's So Good About Biodiversity?: A Call for Better Reasoning About Nature's Value.* New York: Springer, 2012.

Glen Martin   *Game Changer: Animal Rights and the Fate of Africa's Wildlife.* Berkeley: University of California Press, 2012.

Pamela L. Martin   *Oil in the Soil: The Politics of Paying to Preserve the Amazon.* Lanham, MD: Rowman & Littlefield, 2011.

Shahid Naeem et al., eds.   *Biodiversity, Ecosystem Functioning, and Human Wellbeing: An Ecological and Economic Perspective.* New York: Oxford University Press, 2009.

Virginia D. Nazarea   *Heirloom Seeds and Their Keepers: Marginality and Memory in the Conservation of Biological Diversity.* Tucson: University of Arizona Press, 2005.

Richard Pearson   *Driven to Extinction: The Impact of Climate Change on Biodiversity.* New York: Sterling, 2011.

Carol Petrini   *Terra Madre: Forging a New Global Network of Sustainable Food Communities.* White River Junction, VT: Chelsea Green, 2009.

Suresh C. Rai   *Ecotourism and Biodiversity Conservation.* New York: Nova Science Publishers, 2012.

Will Steffan et al.   *Australia's Biodiversity and Climate Change.* Collingwood, Victoria: CSIRO Publishing, 2009.

Harold M. Tyus   *Ecology and Conservation of Fishes.* Boca Raton, FL: CRC Press, 2012.

Index

Geographic headings and page numbers in **boldface** refer to viewpoints about that country or region.

CPSIA information can be obtained
at www.ICGtesting.com
Printed in the USA
FFOW04n0744031013
1958FF